"A supremely important contribu  eadth
of the meaning of the liturgy as a ɔaschal
victory of Christ. Taking the pasc ɪ of
Pentecost as its focus this comme ι death
itself and passing over to new life again and again in Christ through the
celebration of the liturgy."

—Msgr. Kevin Irwin
The Catholic University of America

"In this extraordinarily rich volume, Jeremy Driscoll shows how we
experience the awesome glory of the resurrection in the liturgy of the
Paschal Triduum and the Easter Season. His insightful liturgical exegesis
reveals how the lectionary proclaims a coherent story of God's saving
grace in the crucified and risen Christ. A perfect resource for the Triduum
and the Easter Season!"

—Frank J. Matera
Professor Emeritus
The Catholic University of America

"What more can be said about the resurrection? Yet we must come to
fresh appreciation of this central mystery for the sake of our Christian
faith. What is Christ doing? What are we doing? Abbot Jeremy guides the
reader, flashlight in hand, on a gentle walk through Scripture and Liturgy
conjoined. First the transforming power of resurrection is shown in the
biblical account of the Pasch. Then the Lord's presence and power in the
sacramental signs of the Paschal Triduum is shown. (Who could have
guessed there was so much theology in the rubrics and texts and actions
of these days?) This is liturgical exegesis at its best. Everyone should
make a Lenten spiritual reading retreat by turning to this book during the
last days of Lent and preparing themselves for the mystery of the Paschal
vigil. Abbot Jeremy becomes theologian, poet, homilist, mystagogue, and
spiritual father."

—David W. Fagerberg
Professor, University of Notre Dame

"Abbot Jeremy takes us on a spiritual journey through the most basic belief that gives meaning to our Christian identity—the death and resurrection of Jesus Christ. This book enables us to understand with depth how our life as a Christian is touched by this belief. He shows how profound our lives are touched by the paschal mystery and how the liturgy continues to draw us deeper into the very life of Christ. When read slowly and meditatively, this book is life changing."

—Abbot Gregory J. Polan, OSB
Primate of the Benedictine Confederation, Sant'Anselmo, Rome

Awesome Glory

Resurrection in Scripture, Liturgy, and Theology

Jeremy Driscoll, OSB

LITURGICAL PRESS
Collegeville, Minnesota

www.litpress.org

1	2	3	4	5	6	7	8	9

Library of Congress Cataloging-in-Publication Data

Names: Driscoll, Jeremy, 1951– author.
Title: Awesome glory : resurrection in scripture, liturgy, and theology / Jeremy Driscoll, O.S.B.
Description: Collegeville, Minnesota : Liturgical Press, 2019.
Identifiers: LCCN 2018034339 (print) | LCCN 2018044392 (ebook) | ISBN 9780814644270 (ebook) | ISBN 9780814644034 (pbk.)
Subjects: LCSH: Jesus Christ—Resurrection. | Catholic Church—Doctrines.
Classification: LCC BT482 (ebook) | LCC BT482 .D75 2019 (print) | DDC 232/.5—dc23
LC record available at https://lccn.loc.gov/2018034339

For the monks of Mount Angel Abbey
An effort by their Abbot,
wanting to strengthen their joy and their hope

Contents

Introduction

The most important event of human history, indeed, the most important event that has ever happened anywhere in the created universe, is the death of Jesus Christ on the cross and his being raised from the dead by the one whom he called God and Father. This event is the central proclamation of Christian faith. Everything that is Christian derives from this: a way of life, a way of prayer, a body of doctrine. If we Christians are to understand our faith and live it, we must continually deepen our grasp of what it means to say that the Jesus who was crucified has been raised up. An unimaginable new content has been introduced into our world by the resurrection of Jesus. Everything in the created order is changed by it. What was "natural" can now be played in a new key: a sweeter, stronger music that is nothing less than supernatural. The new key of resurrection takes up every melody of the old creation—from the joyous sounds of life's greatest pleasures to the heartrending cries of suffering and death—and plays it in its supernatural tones. All that was passing and destined to be lost in the natural world is transformed into a song that will sound forever in the presence of God.

Easter is the annual celebration of this totally transformative event. By our very celebration of it—which in fact is extended over many days—we come under its force, we yield to its sway, we are inserted into the new life that will never end. Sunday Eucharist is the weekly celebration of this totally transformative event. Annually, in our celebration of Easter, we are renewed in our participation in the mystery of the Lord's resurrection. Weekly, in our celebration of Sunday Eucharist, we are renewed in the same. Annually we prepare for Easter with forty days of Lent. We enter Easter day by means of the liturgies of the Paschal Triduum, but these launch us into the fifty days of Paschaltide, and all this culminates in the feast of Pentecost, an unimaginable outpouring of the Holy Spirit upon the whole world.

The church lives her whole life in the world from the regular and continual nourishment she receives from her participation in these

1

events. The liturgies of the Paschal Triduum, of the whole paschal season, and of Pentecost, as well as all the subsequent Sundays of the year, are themselves *events*. They are strong, complex sets of rites. In all their moving and acting and speaking and singing and taking up of symbols of the strongest kind, these liturgies become *events* in the community that celebrates them. In fact, these liturgical *events* converge with the most important *event* that has ever happened: the death and resurrection of Jesus. By means of the liturgical events the community has communion in *the* event. We die with Christ and rise with him to new and everlasting life.

With this book, I want to suggest that we are in need of a much clearer focus on the mystery of the Lord's resurrection as the principal content of the Christian message. I do not simply say something to the effect of, "We should sort of emphasize the resurrection a bit more." I want to come to a more foundational level of the question, one that explores the deep structure of the entire Christian message with its center in resurrection. Resurrection is the deep structure and message of each of the *four gospels*. It is the deep structure of the birth of the church as narrated in the *Acts of the Apostles*. All of *Paul's letters* are constructed and move within this same deep structure. "If Christ has not been raised, then empty is our preaching; empty, too, your faith." he exclaims in 1 Corinthians (15:14). Likewise, the *liturgy*, in all its constitutive parts, echoes the same deep structure represented in all these New Testament texts. To take for the moment just the example of the form of the eucharistic liturgy, we see resurrection as the deep structure of the entire *Lectionary*, just as it is the deep structure in the liturgy of the *Eucharist*, which celebrates the memorial of Jesus' entry into his death and glorification by means of his Last Supper.

The better we understand these interpenetrating deep structures, the more mindfully we can participate in them and celebrate them and, indeed, live our whole lives in the world from the new life they bequeath to us. *We* become witnesses to what God has done and is doing still. *We* become evidence in the world that the Jesus who was crucified has been raised up by God, and so all things are new.

A Story from the Synod on New Evangelization

The church held a synod on the new evangelization during three weeks of October 2012, scheduled to coincide with the fiftieth anniversary of the opening of Vatican Council II. This synod and many other things have set the whole Catholic community to thinking further about the new evangelization called for repeatedly by recent popes. It is worth observing that to evangelize well, we must be in renewed and ardent touch with what makes the Gospel compelling to ourselves. Evangelization is always an overflow of something else. Grasping at greater depth and with deeper wonder the absolute and total novelty of the divine deed that raised Jesus from the dead and gives us a share in his new life—this makes the Gospel compelling, and our sharing it with others should overflow from it.

One of the major focuses of the new evangelization is to bring alive again the vigor of the faith in the already baptized who may not be practicing any more or whose practice has grown lukewarm and mediocre. Once grasped and believed in, the actual content of what Christian faith proclaims is something absolutely stunning. I think one of the main tasks of the new evangelization for the whole church is a recovered sense of clarity about what the central core of the proclamation is. That may sound obvious, but I believe we are lacking this clarity in the general day to day of our life together in the church and in many of our pastoral undertakings. This is a theological question that needs to be treated competently and correctly, and it is also a question of the spirituality that would flow from this center correctly and be effectively identified by theology. This book is an attempt to do that.

I would like to share a story from the synod. In his intervention on the floor of the synod hall, addressing the entire assembly of bishops, Cardinal Telesphore Toppo from India told a story. It exactly caught my concerns. He told of a Hindu teenager who had been hanging around the Catholic priests for some time, in a school setting of some sort. I do not remember the details of the setting. But the boy was obviously a spiritual seeker, and he was often asking questions about Christian belief. At one point one of the priests gave the boy a copy of the gospels and told him to read them and then come back with questions and reactions. The boy came back more or less flabbergasted and accusing. He wanted to be sure he had got it right, and so he demanded clarification. "Jesus is risen from the dead?" he asked, "really risen from the dead?" "Yes," they calmly answered, not displeased at his excitement. "Why didn't you tell me!" he shouted at them, astonished that they would not have told him that straight out from the start.

I think this is a big lesson for us all as we consider the new evangelization, a big lesson for us all as we consider what it means to identify ourselves as believing Christians. Surely, that Jesus is risen from the dead is the central point. Everything else flows from that. Of course, there is much more than that to say and think about. But everything flows from resurrection of the crucified Jesus and leads back to that. Resurrection light defuses itself through everything that Christians believe and proclaim and know to say about Jesus.

Something Called "Ping"

I ask my reader's indulgence to offer what perhaps may be considered a poetic interlude in this introduction. I want to express the importance of our pondering the resurrection in this book in a context that takes the whole cosmos into account. Cosmic consequences will not be my main focus in the book, but they are the ultimate context. This is an account of a dream I had that can perhaps evoke the point I want to make about the cosmic context of our thinking together about resurrection. I title my account "Ping." This obscure title will, I hope, come clear with the reading.

"Ping." During a restless night of sleep I had many mini-dreams, most of which, as usual, made no sense. However, there were two that did, one of them curious and interesting; the other, it would seem, a profound illumination. The curious dream was simply being presented with a title, a title which was like that of some symposium or project. It was

The Sun at Its Zenith
Noon in Cosmos and Culture

There it stood in front of me. And I remember thinking, half asleep, half awake: not a bad phrase to come upon in a dream.

The second dream had to do with the cosmic context of the death of Christ, and although there were many nonsensical dreams between the symposium title and this, this dream seemed somehow to derive from the symposium title. Lurking in the back of the dream on the borders of my awareness was the line from the gospels as Jesus was dying: "It was now about noon and darkness came over the whole land" (Luke 23:44).

In this dream there was a vision of tiny planet Earth from far out in the cosmos, from the very edges of our solar system or perhaps beyond it. It was one of the millions of things shining, but somehow I knew it was Earth, planet Earth. Then suddenly it shone with a new ping of light, not outshining any other but pinging with a new light, different from all the rest. I knew—intuition dream—that it was light from the moment of Christ's death, the moment in which the Lord of the Universe, God himself, had undergone that monstrous thing that had come to be on Earth, human death. And by God's having undergone it, it was also in that instant transformed. This was the ping of light. I saw that all the long history of the cosmos, its nearly fourteen billion years, was headed toward this Marvelous Exchange. Not only was this a universe that somehow knew we human beings were coming—we are not merely a monstrous accident of chance and evolution—it was a universe that knew God would make this Exchange, a universe that God made so that this could happen. Death stings and poisons that creature distinguished from all others by its awareness of coming death, but then God comes and makes this Exchange, standing himself in the place of death and so removing its sting. Intuition dream.

Then I awoke into my own little place on this planet floating in the cosmos. Earth, where God raised Jesus from the dead.

The Structure of the Book

There are many ways to think about the mystery of the resurrection. The testimony of *Scripture*, of course, is fundamental. But what the Scriptures recount has been thought about for millennia by believing Christians, and all sorts of *theology* has come about from that. The Scriptures come especially alive when they are proclaimed in the *liturgy*, but they also expand from being words proclaimed into becoming *sacramental events* that totally draw believers up into the mystery of resurrection. Scriptural words become sacraments, and Christians die and rise with Christ in baptism and live from his glorious risen life in the nourishment of the Eucharist. All this makes it possible and, indeed, imperative that *we live in a new way* in the world. The world is meant to be changed radically because of the way Christians live within it their participation in the resurrection. Each of these dimensions (italicized above) suggest both a method and a structure for the book.

Part 1 offers a summary of the proclamation of resurrection in theological terms. I do not begin straightaway with the scriptural witness that is so fundamental to our knowledge of resurrection. I presume my reader has a general knowledge of the basic lines of the claim—namely, that after a brief but spellbinding ministry of preaching and healing, Jesus of Nazareth is misunderstood by the religious authorities of his day and, with the collusion with the Romans and these authorities, is crucified. Later, to the astonishment of those who had followed him and had, because of the crucifixion, thought themselves mistaken for having believed him to be the Messiah, Jesus appeared to chosen witnesses in a glorified state in which he indeed was seen to be Lord and Messiah. On the basis of this fundamental outline of the story, I want in part 1 to pull all the different scriptural ways of speaking about the extraordinary experiences of these chosen witnesses into a single synthetic vision that describes the Christian experience of the resurrection of the crucified Jesus.

When I say resurrection, this is, of course, intimately connected with the crucifixion of Jesus. But no one would be speaking about his crucifixion, much less his preaching and ministry, were it not that God had raised the one who had been crucified from the dead. This intimate connection between cross and resurrection is made clear in all the New Testament texts, however diverse from one another they may be. It is also an intimate connection made manifest in all the liturgies that the Christian community celebrates. The community's liturgical gatherings become the primary context for an encounter in the here and now with the crucified and glorious Lord Jesus. Such gatherings are the context that first created the New Testament texts and in which they are subsequently proclaimed. Such gatherings are also the context of the Lord's presence and power to save through sacramental signs. So part 1 finishes with a presentation of the birth of the liturgy as a constitutive part of the event of the Paschal Mystery itself. This sets us up and leads naturally into part 2.

Part 2 considers the witness to cross and resurrection in the liturgy of the church, not in general terms, but in a focused way on the very heart of the liturgical year—namely, the Paschal Triduum with its climax in the Paschal Vigil and the opening of this into the fifty days of Easter until Pentecost. There are separate chapters on Holy Thursday, Good Friday, the Paschal Vigil, Easter day and its Octave, Ascension, and, finally, Pentecost. These liturgies present us with abundant materials for exploring and deepening our understanding of resurrection. From these liturgies—from the Scriptures proclaimed in them and the rituals enacted—the church's rich theological understanding has developed. But not only that. These liturgies effectively establish us in communion with the death and resurrection of Jesus in such a way that we can live in the world with the Spirit-filled energy that is given us by these. Reflecting on these liturgies will require of us what could be called a *liturgical exegesis;* that is, a discussion of passages of Scripture that takes account of their place in the liturgy, in relation to the other passages in that liturgy and in relation to the sacramental realities celebrated there.

I regret that I cannot do more than this in the present book, for there will be a great deal left untouched. The next move—another book?—in the logic of the method and structure I am using would be to examine, especially by means of the deeply theological letters of St. Paul, the consequences of resurrection for us and how we live. Paul's theology teaches us that the resurrection of Jesus is an event with universal consequences for the whole of humanity and the cosmos. It likewise has moral consequences that equip believers to live in a completely different way, not according to the flesh but according to the Spirit. Resurrection creates a community of believers called in turn *church, temple of the Holy Spirit, Body of Christ.*

A note to the reader on how I will speak of the various liturgies. I imagine them beautifully celebrated according to the ideal that the liturgical books themselves set down. This way of speaking is an invitation not to get snagged for the moment on practical problems or unfortunate ways of celebrating that we may have encountered. To develop a theology based on the liturgical experience, the liturgical experience has to be imagined in its ideal form.

In any case, it is time now to dive in and do what we can. "Jesus is risen from the dead?" the little Hindu boy asked his Christian friends. "Why didn't you tell me?" Let us see if we can deepen our own understanding, hoping that no one will ever reproach us with such a question.

Part 1

A Summary
of the Proclamation in
Theological Terms

The event of Jesus' death and resurrection is the central proclamation of Christian faith. But this event, in fact, unfolds into
infinite dimensions. By means of this event, God reveals who
God is and what his plan and intentions are in having created the
world. The theological tradition has developed an expression that
enables us to say all at once: death, resurrection, ascension, sending
of the Spirit, and establishing of the church. The expression *Paschal
Mystery* means all of this at once, all of this as one single, huge deed
of God posited in our world. It is important for us to understand the
logic of this claim, that all these various events are essentially one
huge event, something that can be named with a single expression.
Jesus himself named it with a single expression, calling it "my hour"
on a number of occasions, as reported in the Gospel of John (John 2:4;
5:25, 28; 7:30; 8:20; 12:13; 17:1), and the evangelist himself uses this
same term for the multilayered reality (John 13:1). Jesus also refers to
his cross, resurrection, and ascension by the single term of his being
"lifted up" (John 3:14; 8:28; 12:34).

Understanding the logic of using single expressions—*Paschal Mystery, hour, being lifted up*—for these various events is the task of part
1. There are four little chapters here. First, the Paschal Mystery as a
whole will be described, drawing into a unified vision, language from
Scripture, theology, and liturgy. Second, we will look more closely at

the range of meanings in the word *pasch*, hoping thereby to heighten our sensibilities to the words *pasch* and *paschal* as these are used in Scripture, theology, and the liturgy. Third, we will reflect in theological terms on the nature of the crisis that the community of Jesus' disciples experienced at his death. Tightly joined to this, we will speak also in theological terms of how this crisis is unexpectedly overcome in the community's encounters with Jesus risen from the dead. In a fourth chapter, we see that the origins of the liturgies that we still celebrate today are rooted in the paschal event itself, that liturgy is an actual part or dimension of Jesus being raised from the dead.

Chapter 1

The Paschal Mystery Described

In the several years of ministry before his passion and death, Jesus of Nazareth gathered a group of disciples around himself and moved with them through Galilee announcing that the kingdom of God is at hand. People were spellbound by his teaching. He worked wonderful signs of healing. And when his closest disciples began to believe him to be the Messiah promised by God who would restore the kingdom to Israel, he taught them that the Messiah had to go up to Jerusalem, suffer greatly from the elders, the chief priests, and the scribes, then be killed and on the third day be raised up. This mysterious teaching was not understood at the time, but Jesus continued to repeat it to his disciples. As his ministry advanced, Jesus revealed himself to be totally caught up and marked by this strange messianic vision. He set his face to go up to Jerusalem. And we would not be wrong to consider his ministry of teaching and healing to be a slow and determined procession to Jerusalem, where he was ready to undergo what awaited him.

At every stage of his ministry Jesus showed himself to be totally shaped by his confident surrender to the One whose coming kingdom he announced, the kingdom of his God and Father. His disciples found him absorbed in prayer through the long hours of the night or in the early hours of the morning. One of the most precious gifts he gave them was teaching them how to pray as he did, by addressing God with the close and affectionate title of *Abba*, Father. Jesus spoke constantly of his Father, and he revealed who God is by speaking in marvelous parables of the Father's love. On the occasions when he spoke of the signs of healing that he worked, he explained that he did them because he had been sent from his Father, that he and the Father were one, that he did only what he saw the Father doing (John 5:16-47).

Jesus' constant surrender to his Father, which characterized his entire life, culminated in his death on the cross, when he entrusted himself entirely into the hands of the One who alone could save him. The gospels give us glimpses of how profound was the agony of Jesus in the last hours of his life, to the point even of sweating drops of blood. But he kept on praying and called God "Abba" and said, "Abba, Father . . . not what I will but what you will" (Mark 14:36). And even if in the course of the long, drawn-out hours of his dying, he was heard to pray "My God, my God, why have you forsaken me?" (Matt 27:46), his very last words were "Father, into your hands I commend my spirit" (Luke 23:46) and "It is finished" (John 19:30). Praying thus, he uttered a loud cry and passed over his spirit. Jesus' whole life was a procession toward that loud cry, where with his body even more than his voice, he thrust his whole being toward the One whose coming reign he announced, toward the One who alone could save him.

Jesus' cry was answered by the Father. When Jesus surrendered himself completely to God in death, then God the Father surrendered himself completely to his Son, filling him with divine life, raising him up from the dead, making him the first human being born again from the dead and thus making him the pioneer of our salvation. Jesus' whole life, culminating in his death, was an invocation of God with the name "Father." God answers this invocation with an invocation of his own. "Beloved Son!" he says to Jesus. And the uttering of this name raises him up. This exchange of names is the highpoint of all the deeds of God in the created universe. This exchange *is* the death of Jesus and his resurrection, his death conceived as his crying out the name "Father" with his entire being, his resurrection conceived as the Father's crying out "Beloved Son" with his entire being (see Acts 13:33).

This exchange of names has occurred from all eternity. It is what God *is*. But what is new here—utterly unforeseen, completely un-dreamed of—is that this exchange of names should take place now, at a particular place and time in the created universe, indeed that it should take place from within the realm of death, that realm set up by rebellious creation which had ruptured the relationship with God, the exchange of names that God wished to share between himself and human beings. If the exchange of divine names can occur even within the realm of death, this means that the power of that realm is undone. Its continued power—that we all must undergo death—is henceforth only apparent, for what happened at Jesus' death cannot pass away. From within the space of death Jesus said "Father," and into that realm the Father pronounced the name "Beloved Son." All of us who must enter that realm can now do so crying out the name "Father" in confident surrender, and we can expect to hear ourselves addressed there by a name which raises us up: "Beloved!" But I am perhaps getting ahead of myself. I am talking already about our share in the Paschal Mystery. We have not yet finished watching that immense event unfold. Let us turn back to it, knowing that we can come in due time to a careful meditation of all the ways we share in it.

Raising Jesus from the dead was but the beginning of the Father's answer to his Son's surrender into his hands. The Father glorified his Son totally and absolutely. The risen Son ascended into heaven in his glorified body, drawing the whole universe toward him in this luminous ascent, for he is connaturally joined in his body to the whole created realm. The ascended Son was seated in glory at the Father's right hand. To say something like this—seated at God's right hand—is language and an image with which we grope for some way to say that Jesus is placed totally where God is, that he completely shares all that is of God, the Father Almighty, creator of heaven and earth, of all things visible and invisible. But if in his glorification Jesus is seated now at the Father's right hand, we can never forget or stop being amazed that the one who is seated there is the one who was crucified. Ascended into heaven and glorified forever at his Father's right hand, Jesus gives unceasing thanks and praise for his having been raised up, for his own glorification. His crucified and now glorified body retains the wounds of his crucifixion. Those wounds are continually set before the Father's eyes. They continue to plead on our behalf. His wounds call upon the Father to send forth on the rest of humanity the Spirit that raised him from the dead.

The Spirit that raised Jesus from the dead—this is another way, another angle from which to view the jewel of the Paschal Mystery. The *Father* filled with his *Breath (the Spirit)* the corpse of his *Son*. The risen Lord breathed on his disciples and said to them, "Receive the holy Spirit" (John 20:22)! The Spirit given to Jesus at his resurrection immediately flowed through him to those who believed in him. The gift of the Father, then, was enormous. Not only was his glorified Son in their midst, but the Spirit immediately flowed out through him. Yet there seem to be stages, as it were, of the revelation of this infinite gift. For forty days the disciples' attention was focused on encounters with the risen Jesus, meeting him in that same body in which he was crucified, "eating and drinking with him after he rose from the dead" (see Acts 10:41). But after forty days Jesus was taken from their sight as he ascended into heaven, after telling his disciples to wait in Jerusalem for the gift of the Holy Spirit that he had promised.

On Pentecost, suddenly the Holy Spirit came down with force on the gathered disciples. What in fact is happening here, what this reveals, is that the Father's act of raising Jesus in the Spirit is inseparably one with his act of transmitting the Spirit through Jesus to all who believe in him. This outpouring of the Spirit from the Father through the body of the ascended Lord Jesus is nothing less than the birth of the church, that is, the birth of a community of disciples who are filled in their mortal bodies with the same Spirit that raised Jesus from the dead. This Spirit renders these disciples capable of understanding all that God has done in raising Jesus from the dead. The Spirit makes them witnesses and forceful preachers whose announcement of the deed of God becomes the very occasion of the hearers encountering the risen Lord whom the disciples announce. So, just as the Father's raising of the Son is inseparably one with his sending of the Spirit, the sending of the Spirit is inseparably one with the birth of the church. All this, from the death of Jesus to the birth of the church, *is* the Paschal Mystery. It is his hour. It is his being lifted up, when he draws all things to himself. It is an hour which does not pass away. Each of the Paschal Mystery's dimensions is inseparably one with the other.

It is striking how, in order to speak of all the dimensions of the death and resurrection of Jesus, we have had to speak of Father, Son, and Holy Spirit and also of the church. The death and resurrection of Jesus *is* the revelation of the Holy Trinity, which includes our communion in trinitarian life. And although it would take us too far afield to enter at length into a discussion of the doctrine of the Holy Trinity, it is important for us to realize that the doctrine has its roots here. In other words, the doctrine of the Trinity is not some arbitrarily complex and too subtle a set of ideas about God. It is rather how the community that encounters God through the resurrection of Jesus learns to speak of all that God is—knowledge of God inconceivable without all that is revealed in the Paschal Mystery.

We have just mentioned how the outpouring of the Holy Spirit at Pentecost created a body of disciples capable of understanding what God had done in raising Jesus from the dead. They were not only granted a new level of understanding, but they also became fearless in witnessing to it. The Acts of the Apostles leaves us the precious record of many of the sermons of the Spirit-filled witnesses. Again and again, we hear variations on one basic, core announcement that constitutes the central content of their message. In one way or another they announce, "This Jesus who was crucified, God has raised him up, and we are his witnesses."

Chapter 2

The Range of Meanings in the Word *Pasch*

We have seen in effect that the expression *Paschal Mystery* is used by theology as a sort of shorthand term to summarize many dimensions of a single immense deed of God, the center of which is Jesus' death and resurrection. But why is the word *paschal* used to describe and summarize this deed of God? There is a remarkable range of meanings that swirl around the various words Christians have used to describe and proclaim the overwhelming and unexpected event of Jesus' death and resurrection. And what those words mean changes slightly from one language to another: from Aramaic to Hebrew to Greek to Latin and then to our modern languages. One of the most important words for our purposes is the word *Pasch* and its adjective *paschal.* If we can trace something of what this word has meant through the Christian centuries, it will deepen our own understanding of what the word can mean for us as we use it today.

The words *pasch* and *paschal* ultimately derive from the Aramaic form of the Hebrew word *pesach*, which became *pascha* in Greek and Latin. And we usually render the Hebrew term in English as *Passover*, the name of the great Jewish feast. But English is tricky here, because if someone were to ask how to say "Passover" in French or Italian or Spanish, the answer would be *Pâques* or *Pasqua* or *Pascua*—words all clearly based on the same root as the Greek and Latin *Pascha.* But if you ask how to say "Easter" in these languages, the answer would be the same: *Pâques* or *Pasqua* or *Pascua.* English thus has two different words, *Passover* and *Easter.* With the English word *Passover,* Jews and

Christians alike refer to the great Jewish feast. With *Easter,* we think of the Sunday of Jesus' resurrection.

Something is lost for us in English by this double terminology. Not only do the modern Romance languages have one single term for the Jewish and Christian feast, but this was also the case in ancient Greek and Latin. For Jew and Christian alike, in all these languages, it was the great *Pascha.* As such, the term could include a great deal. It meant the Jewish feast of Passover in all its dimensions, the annual memorial in which the Jewish community recounted in joyful feasting the wonderful deeds whereby God had led his people out of Egypt with his mighty outstretched arm. For Christians, the death and resurrection of Jesus is an event which, by God's own design, took place within the heart of the Jewish feast. The Jewish feast is consequently seen to be a prophecy, now fulfilled, of Jesus' death and resurrection. He transforms the feast. His death and resurrection is a new and definitive Passover, a new and definitive *Pascha.* But it should be noted that one word, one feast, holds both death and resurrection together. Together they are *Pascha.*

This marvelous mystery, this marvelous understanding, of death and resurrection so inextricably bound up with one another, can be weakened by the way we use the word *Easter* in English. (The same problem is found with the related word and usage in German and Dutch, for example.) For the word *Easter* means for us the day of resurrection, and it carries little or nothing of the tension of death that the word *pascha* contains. It can cause us, for example, to think of the Easter Triduum (in Latin this is *triduum paschale*) as occurring in separate, distinct phases: first death, then resurrection. But in fact the liturgy, not to mention the events themselves of which it is a memorial, is not so neatly and simply divided up as that. Rather, it moves in concentric circles, each day of the Triduum advancing toward resurrection, celebrating it somehow already from the very start, and then circling back to recall again, all the way through to the end, some dimension of the Lord's death, which is itself already glorious. That the Lord's death and resurrection occurred in the course of the Jewish *Pascha* and was seen to be its new and definitive meaning— this gave rise to an annual celebration for Christians of Christ's new and definitive *Pascha. Pascha* was the feast of the Lord's death and resurrection, one feast celebrated in a Triduum, one feast with many dimensions, dimensions which unfold in the various liturgies of the

Triduum, just as the events of Jesus' death and resurrection unfolded as one huge deed of God.

In the long run, then, we can see that it makes a difference whether we call the Triduum the Easter Triduum or the Paschal Triduum, whether we call the great Vigil the Easter Vigil or the Paschal Vigil. For example, if we call it the Easter Vigil, we are immediately geared to reading the movement, the signs, the words of the liturgy as a liturgy which moves from death to resurrection. If we call it the Paschal Vigil (as the original Latin does: *vigilia paschalis*), we are better prepared in fact to see how subtle and profound this liturgy is, precisely because it does not move in a simple line from death to resurrection but rather is a magnificent, complex liturgy which holds together in a kind of glorious tension all the interpenetrating dimensions of the Lord's death and resurrection and these together with death and resurrection in the sacrament of baptism and these together with death and resurrection in the Eucharist.

We will speak about this more at length in part 2 when we discuss these and other liturgies. But I use the example of how we may or may not experience these liturgies now in order to render precise the point, from the very beginning of these reflections, that death and resurrection are inextricably intertwined—in the nature of the event itself, in the scriptural accounts, in the experience of the disciples, and in our own encounter with the same through the liturgy. The one word *paschal* holds this mysterious intertwining in perfect balance and tension.

Of course, I am not suggesting that we should somehow suddenly try to do without the word *Easter* in English. That would be unnatural. It is a word filled with wonderful content and connotations for all of us. For after all, its meaning is that the Lord is risen. I have entered into this perhaps slightly technical discussion not so much to dislodge *Easter* from our vocabulary as to explain the stronger sense of the connotations of the words *Pasch* and *paschal*. These are words that we must be able to use if we want to plumb the full depths of the liturgical traditions in which we celebrate, traditions developed in Latin and Greek, traditions in which the one word *Pascha* means the death and resurrection of the Lord. In what follows, I will use both the term *Pasch* and the more familiar English word *Passover* to remind the reader that these are the same word in the original languages.

The importance of this becomes clearer if we look briefly at some of the broad lines of the historical development of the Christian celebration of Pasch in the early centuries of the community's existence. Not surprisingly, different communities in different geographical areas developed their own understanding and emphases in the celebration of the feast. These are complimentary understandings, and they converge into the form of the celebration as we know it today. We are the rich heirs of various theological currents.

Two thousand years of the history of liturgy around this question is a lot. Nonetheless, scholars of this topic represent the vast material well by observing that there are two fundamental trends in what the feast celebrated. These could be called Pasch as *passion* and Pasch as *passage*. These two dimensions are already present within Israel's own understanding of Passover, represented respectively in Exodus 12 and Exodus 14.

Exodus 12, representing *Pasch as passion*, describes the prescriptions for the slaughtering and eating of the paschal lamb. Its blood is to be spread on the doorposts and lintels of the Israelites' houses, and they are to eat its roasted flesh together. We hear the Lord's own solemn words naming the feast and defining the meaning of this name. He says, "It is the Passover [in Hebrew, *pesach*] of the LORD. For on this same night I will go through Egypt, striking down every firstborn of the land . . ." And then he adds, "But the blood will mark the houses where you are. Seeing the blood, I will pass over you" (Exod 12:11-13). In this sense of the word *Passover*, it is the Lord himself who passes. He passes through the land striking down the firstborn, and he passes over the houses marked with the lamb's blood. Because the lamb's blood was what protected the houses of the Israelites, this can be called Pasch as passion, protection intimately connected with the slaughtering of a lamb.

If, as I said, early Christians were struck by the fact that Jesus' death and resurrection took place deep inside the celebration of this paschal feast and meal, it is not difficult to see why they would use images of the meal—with the slaughtered lamb, its blood as protection, its roasted flesh feeding the family—to understand no longer the Jewish *pesach* but the new Pasch accomplished in Jesus' death and resurrection. This became an annual celebration for Christians, just as the Jewish Passover was an annual celebration. And for some several centuries in many Christian lands, this celebration was observed on the very same day as the Jewish Passover and not, as we do now, on the Sunday that follows Passover, or more precisely, on a Triduum that climaxes on the Sunday following Passover.

Christians who celebrated according to this usage, strongly shaped by the images of Exodus 12 in their understanding of the Lord's death and resurrection, were called by what may seem to us a somewhat intimidating name: Quartodecimans. We might translate this as "Fourteeners," meaning that they were characterized by their celebration of the Christian Pasch on the fourteenth day of Nisan, the day prescribed for the celebration of the Jewish Passover. Odd names aside, this community's celebration was full of profound insights into the mystery of the death and resurrection of Jesus. We would be hard-pressed to capture this richness, however, if we simply referred to this as their celebration of *Easter.* Again, this gears us to think of them as primarily celebrating the resurrection. In the end, of course, theologically this is so. But we should observe the striking way in which they arrived at that. Their celebration of Pasch very much emphasized the Lord's suffering and death, of which the paschal lamb was the image. Pasch for them was memory and celebration of the Lord's glorious and life-giving death, where blood that saves us was shed, where from the cross the slaughtered Lamb gives us his flesh to eat. Christ is the Lamb of God who takes away the sins of the world! This is Pasch as passion.

The other major current, *Pasch as passage,* develops differently from this. After many centuries it converges, as I said, with the other, creating the rich liturgies of which we are now the heirs. But let us look for a moment at the origins of the development of this current. Here the decisive influence is Exodus 14, the marvelous account of Israel's exodus from Egypt and its crossing through the Red Sea. This too was call *pesach* by the Jewish people, but now the sense of the word emphasizes not so much *the Lord's* passing over (as in Exodus 12) as *the people's* passing over: their passing over from Egypt to the desert where they would enter a covenant with God on Sinai. And this would ultimately lead to their passing over the Jordan into the Promised Land. Of course, according to the biblical account, the people were able to get as far as the sea and beyond it because first the blood of the Lamb had protected them and permitted their leaving. So in effect we are talking about one complex event, called *Pesach.* But in fact, in communities of Christians different from the Quartodecimans, the images of Exodus 14 exercised a greater influence on how they understood, remembered, and celebrated the Lord's death and resurrection.

It is not difficult to see how this could be so. Again, struck by the fact that Jesus' death and resurrection occurred during the Jewish celebration of this marvelous passage of the Red Sea, Christians could not help but view what the Jewish feast celebrated as only a prophecy of a passage greater than which none could be conceived: Jesus' passage from death to life, from this world to the Father. And this is a passage which he invites us all to make with him. So it is not just he who passes, but all the people pass over. Thus, in this tradition, Egypt represents the slavery of sin and death; the turbulent waters of the sea are sin and death threatening to devour the people (the terrors of the grave, as it were); the passage to the other side is the new life of Jesus' resurrection in which all who pass over with him share, the other side of the tomb. Again, one word describes all these dimensions; one word describes both sides of the sea, the side on which the Egyptians are near and still threatening the people, and the other side where the people are safe on the opposite shore, with the Egyptians and their chariots drowned behind them. This is Pasch; both sides are Pasch. Christ has led us through the waters of the deep, and we have come up the other side where, under his leadership, we chant a new song:

I will sing to the LORD, for he is gloriously triumphant;
horse and chariot he has cast into the sea. (Exod 15:1)

This is Pasch as passage.

The Triduum liturgies are a wonderful, intricate web of paschal themes taken from Exodus 12 and 14 and played anew in their Christian key, seeing the death and resurrection of Jesus as the definitive Pasch. As mentioned, examining this in greater detail will be the task of part 2. But even now we can use what the liturgy expresses so eloquently as part of the synthetic theological summary we intend to construct here in part 1. If we are to understand more deeply the event of Jesus' death and resurrection, the scriptural witness to this event, and our own communion in it, then from the start we need to be mindful of the intricate web of paschal themes as both passion and passage. We shall be able to do so the better if we can employ in our vocabulary the wide-ranging sense of the ancient words *Pasch* and *paschal*.

Chapter 3

The Crisis of the Cross and
the Transforming Power of Resurrection

When we say *resurrection*, another way of saying this is the *mystery of the cross*, in which the Lord of glory is hid (see 1 Cor 2:7). The one who is risen is the crucified Messiah. The resurrection opens the mystery of the cross and reveals the glory that is already contained in the Lord's death. But the death of Jesus was not understood by his disciples during the time the events that brought it about were unfolding. Instead, it provoked an enormous crisis in the band of disciples. We should think about the fact that we know of this crisis from those who would announce the resurrection to us, from the disciples of Jesus. This is striking. That the disciples all fled and abandoned Jesus, that Peter denied him three times, that they were hiding behind locked doors after his burial, that on the very morning of his resurrection two disciples were making their way to a village named Emmaus and were speaking of their disappointed hopes in him—all this is not information that somehow unfortunately got out and regrettably puts the disciples in a bad light. No, all this is part of the announcement of the resurrection, given us by the very people who had denied him and fled.

The perspective of the gospels is from resurrection to cross to resurrection. That is to say, if the chronology of the story obviously moves from death to resurrection, the vantage point of its telling is resurrection; and resurrection light is diffused across all the stories that the evangelists tell, beginning from Jesus' birth and even before it and passing through every dimension of his ministry.

This means that the substantial length of the passion accounts of each of the four evangelists and the crisis that the death of Jesus provoked in his disciples must form an essential part of our understanding of the mystery of resurrection. I am talking here about the deep structures of the mystery, structures on which we must continually seek to strengthen our grasp.

The Crisis of the Cross for the Community of Jesus' Disciples

The crisis in the disciples can be summarized in three questions, and I want to suggest that the pattern of struggle revealed in these questions is the pattern of struggle that believers in Jesus today still must undergo. The questions provoked by the death of Jesus on the cross are, first, *Who is God?*; then, *Who is Jesus, who really is Jesus?*; and finally, *What is to become of us, his disciples?* Let us pose each of these questions a little more sharply, in such a way as to make clear what the crisis was.

Who is God if he could have abandoned somebody like Jesus, who had lived his whole life in a faithful turning toward God, in announcing his coming reign? How could God abandon to such a shameful death a man as good and as faithful as Jesus, a spellbinding preacher and a worker of miracles that showed God was surely with him?

Who is Jesus, who saw this hour of his death approaching and did not flee from it? "No one takes [my life] from me," he said. "I have power to lay it down, and power to take it up again" (John 10:18). And what was he revealing in the sign he made at the supper the night before he died? "This is my body, which will be given for you. . . . This cup is the new covenant in my blood, which will be shed for you" (Luke 22:19-20). What enabled him to walk with such freedom, with such love, and with such trust toward such a horrible death?

And what is to become of us, the disciples asked, if Jesus is dead? Will we not face his same fate if we remain together? All the primary relations of the disciples' lives are put in question by the death of Jesus: their new relation with God given them through the preaching and teaching of Jesus; their relation with Jesus, to whom they were deeply attracted and whom they believed to be the Messiah; their relation with one another as the band of his disciples.[1]

---

1. I am inspired in the formulation of this paragraph and these questions by Benoit Standaert, *Lo spazio Gesù: Esperienza, relazione, consegna* (Rome: Ancora, 2004), 247ff.

The four gospels are relatively discrete in what they reveal to us of the interior experience of Jesus during his trial and during the long hours of his agonizing death on the cross. We will examine shortly some of the details they provide us. Yet before looking at what the death of Jesus itself may have been, we can first say something of how it was experienced by the community of his followers. This community had come into being entirely centered on the person of Jesus. Its members were his disciples who believed him to be the Messiah who was going to restore the kingdom of God. Jesus had gathered these disciples by the strength of his preaching, his gestures of kindness, and acceptance of others, especially of those considered to be sinners. He worked marvelous miracles that showed that in him God was visiting his people and that the reign of God was at hand. He was gentle and humble, and people flocked to him for this reason.

We can perhaps deepen the significance of this description of the community of Jesus' disciples if we use the word *body* in several different ways to summarize what was just said. Jesus gathered around himself a *body* of disciples by means of a radiance and attraction that came forth from his own *body*. Where his *body* was, there too was the *body* of his disciples. When Jesus is arrested in the Garden of Gethsemane, his *body* is seized; and this has a reverse effect on the *body* of disciples. When Jesus' *body* is taken away, the *body* of disciples disperses. "I will strike the shepherd, / and the sheep will be dispersed" (Mark 14:27, quoting Zech 13:7).

This separation of the *body* of Jesus and the *body* of his disciples is deepened with agonizing intensity as life in the *body* of Jesus slowly drains from him as he dies on the cross. Jesus is alone in his *body*. *No-body* is with him. And once he is dead and taken down from the cross, then his dead *body*, his corpse, is, among other things, a horrible revelation of the state of his community, the *body* of his disciples. Jesus is truly dead. His *body* is motionless and silent, drained of all radiance and power to attract. Death has cut his *body* off from all further relationship with what had been the *body* of his disciples. There is nothing to do but to bury his *body* in a tomb.

As for his disciples, can we still speak of a *body* of disciples? They are dispersed and in hiding, very naturally fearing for their own lives. One of the gospels gives us the image of them hiding together behind locked doors, waiting for their chance to slip away, to escape from Jerusalem, to return to Galilee from whence they had come. Then perhaps each could return to a former way of life—no longer the *body* of Jesus' disciples, for with the death of his *body*, they no longer had a reason for remaining together. While the disciples of Jesus are hiding behind locked doors, the *body* of Jesus has been consigned to a tomb. We can meditate on the pathos, the drama, expressed in the simultaneity of these two scenes: the *lifeless body* of Jesus in a tomb, the *lifeless body* of his disciples hiding behind locked doors. No one could envision any future life for either of these bodies.

But then something odd occurs, something unforeseen, something not to be looked for in these circumstances. In fact, the *body* of Jesus' disciples does not ultimately disperse. It remains together or comes together again. Just when the death of the *body* of Jesus should have had the result also of the death of the *body* of disciples, that *body* showed itself to be very much alive. The crisis experienced around Jesus' death is unexpectedly overcome.

What happened? What could explain this? We would not be wrong to use the word *resurrection* to describe what happened to the *body* of disciples. The resurrection of the *body* of disciples leads us to the resurrection of the *body* of Jesus. The transformed *body* of disciples is the first evidence we have of the transformed *body* of Jesus. It is not that the *body* of disciples keeps itself together on its own strength and determination. The *body* of disciples does not rise "first," as it were, and then produce a story about the resurrection of Jesus that is a way of keeping his memory alive. Rather, the resurrection of Jesus' *body* immediately invades somehow the *body* of his disciples, filling them with joy and wonder as they share with him the glory and life of God that has filled and raised up the *body* of Jesus. The *body* of disciples is a *body*, a community, of witnesses that God raised Jesus from the dead and filled his *body* with divine glory.

Is it possible to describe, at least to some extent, how all this came about? What happened?

The Fearful, Disbanded Body of Disciples Becomes Fearless Witnesses of Resurrection. What Happened?

It is impossible to reconstruct the details of what exactly happened in the resurrection of Jesus. Questions like "what time?," "what did it look like?," "did it make any noise?," "where did his body go?," "what about clothes?," "what about food?"—these are impossible to answer because the reality of resurrection transcends them all. But there is concrete historical evidence for one thing: it is beyond doubt that the *body* of disciples is completely transformed. Why? What happened to them?

One way of entering into some understanding of this is to note that their relationships are completely reestablished around the three questions proposed by the shock of Jesus' death. The disciples have received a completely new and unexpected relationship with God, with Jesus, and with one another. They have assimilated the shock of Jesus' death at the same depth at which they were struck and dismayed by it. We see evidence of what they experienced in the various kinds of languages of the New Testament, which will be examined in greater detail in part 2. At present it is enough to note that these languages can be roughly categorized as being of three kinds.

There is, first, the language that recounts appearances of the risen Lord to the disciples. These are found mainly in the four gospels, which offer us the basic narrative structures of the event of death and resurrection as we know it. But Acts also speaks of the risen Lord in conversation with his disciples and ascending into heaven in their sight. In Acts we hear also of appearances of the risen Lord in another form to St. Paul. Second, we find the language of brief formulas of confession of faith, of announcing the message: "God raised [Jesus] from the dead" (Rom 10:9). "Jesus is Lord" (1 Cor 12:3). "Christ has been raised from the dead" (1 Cor 15:20). "The Lord has truly been raised and has appeared to Simon!" (Luke 24:34). "Jesus Christ is Lord" (Phil 2:11). "Come, Lord Jesus!" (Rev 22:20). And so on. These are found in the gospels, in Acts, in the letters of the apostles, in the book of Revelation—in short, in every kind of text of the New Testament. Third, there is language that recounts experiences of the Holy Spirit, almost always in groups. Pentecost is the most obvious example, but all experiences of the Holy Spirit should be immediately associated with the resurrection of Jesus. They are its further unfolding.

These three types of communication enable us to understand something of what happened between the death of Jesus and the fearless reappearance of the disciples. Nonetheless, we cannot reconstruct the events as if in a film. The quality of the event itself, its entirely new order, does not permit its being known in that way. Resurrection is not as easy as "Darn, he was dead. Oh good! Now he's back." Resurrection is much more than Jesus of Nazareth being "up and running again." His resurrection is known entirely in its effect in the community, in the *body* of disciples, and in the way the community speaks of what has happened. His resurrection is known and can be known nowhere else but in the community, that is, in the church. Jesus lives his risen life in the *body* of his disciples, filling them more and more with the divine life by which the Father raised him up, filling the world more and more through them. This is not to say that the community invents what happens or that the community keeps itself alive on the strength of its own determination, a sheer willpower to remain together. "Resurrection" is not some vivid first-century Jewish way of saying "we will never forget this wonderful rabbi; let's stick together and remember him." No, rather resurrection is the witnessing to what *God* has done and to what never could have been expected. It is a divine deed, infinite in its proportions.

So we come again to the three questions that described so sharply the crisis of the disciples at the death of Jesus, and we see that each of them is answered in the resurrection of Jesus. Who is God? Who is Jesus? Who are we, his disciples? Resurrection answers: *God* is the one who did not abandon his Son to death. *Jesus* is the one raised by his Father and established as Lord and Messiah. And we? *We* are his witnesses.

The resurrection of Jesus, the divine deed to which the disciples give testimony, is an event of an entirely new order, an event of a different kind, and consequently not able to be experienced as other events in the old order of space and time. Indeed, it involves space and time, it involves *bodies;* but it pulls space and time and *bodies* into a new realm, a realm which establishes its own terms of how it can be known.

In fact, this utterly new deed of God that is the resurrection of Jesus comes to be known in the moment of its announcement. From those originating events in the apostolic community all the way down to the present, to our own day, a same pattern can still be seen—namely, that it is impossible to announce in faith and give witness to the event of the resurrection without the reality and force of resurrection eventually exploding into the present moment of both speaker and hearer. The risen Lord is always present in the word that bears witness to his resurrection.

All the New Testament texts tell us this in many different ways. But so also does any celebration of the liturgy in our own times. For this reason we need to examine the scriptural texts and how these are proclaimed in the liturgy. We need to examine also the ritual actions that accompany these liturgical proclamations of the Word. We need to conduct a liturgical exegesis. What happens when the liturgy is celebrated? Resurrection happens. It is when the message is proclaimed, both in word and in sacrament, that the risen Lord shows himself to be alive and to be alive in the *body* of his disciples. So, our experience of the risen Lord is no less fresh and no less powerful than that of the original community that experienced the same. Through stories of his appearances, through brief formulas of announcement (Jesus is risen!), through the Holy Spirit coming down upon us when we gather as disciples—in all these ways our community today reveals itself to be in direct continuity with the apostolic community, that is, with that *body* of disciples that should have disbanded at the death of Jesus but instead is made one *body* with the *body* of its risen Lord, who invades with his divine glory and lordship his disciples and makes them one *body* with himself.

In apostolic times and still in our times, this community of witnesses is called *Body* of Christ. In apostolic times and still in our times, this community celebrates a memorial of the Lord's death and resurrection, in which the eucharistic *Body* of the Lord reveals the risen Lord as present in a transfigured and glorified *body* whose presence makes all believers one *body* with him. In apostolic times and still in our times, the Holy Spirit is completely poured out on the community that makes the eucharistic memorial of the Lord's death and resurrection. This experience of the Spirit is both the *form* and the *content* of the resurrection announcement. It is *form* in that the Spirit is *how* we know. It is *content* in that the Spirit is *what* we know, *whom* we know, the Spirit who enables us to say of the once-crucified Jesus with our whole being, "Jesus is Lord," and in so doing to say, as he did upon awaking in resurrection, "Abba, Father" to God.

Chapter 4

The Paschal Mystery Celebrated in the Liturgy

We have seen that the Paschal Mystery is something that has its roots in a particular time and place. It is an event within human history: the crucifixion of Jesus Christ under Pontius Pilate. But this event unfolds into dimensions that transcend the historical particulars. The resurrection of Jesus, his glorification at the right hand of the Father, and the sending of the Spirit are all ways in which the particular dimensions of the historical event are transcended. What God has done in Jesus in one time and place becomes available in every time and place. This is God's own doing, and it comes about through the liturgy.

What happens through the celebration of liturgy is part of the Father's glorification of Jesus, part of his gift of resurrection to the Son, where he answers the Son's prayer that all those who will believe in him through his disciples' preaching may be one with him in the glory of the Father (see John 17:20). So, far from being a mere human invention, the liturgy is something that flows forth from within the divine wellspring of the Paschal Mystery. This is seen, above all, in baptism and Eucharist. These sacraments are given us by the Lord himself and given from within the very core of the event of his Paschal Mystery. Jesus gives us the Eucharist as he enters into the hour of his suffering. His command "Do this in memory of me" establishes it as a means in every generation of entering with him into that same hour. And the risen Lord, as he appears in glory before his disciples on the mountain in Galilee, commands them to make disciples of all nations and baptize them in the name of the Father, the Son, and the

Holy Spirit. This command is accompanied by his promise, "And behold, I am with you always, until the end of the age" (Matt 28:20).

The Christian community has been faithful to these injunctions of the Lord in every age. It has been precisely in the celebration of baptism and Eucharist (and in all the other liturgies of the church which in fact group themselves around these) that the community discovered that the Lord had hidden an enormous treasure within the simple rites that he himself handed on to us. He had hidden nothing less than his own presence and power as risen Lord. When the community celebrated these rites, he the Lord was present to all its members and acting to save them, acting to bring them into the risen and glorified life which was his Father's gift to him. After the Lord Jesus had ascended into heaven, disappearing from sight, he sent from the Father the promised gift of the Spirit. This Spirit was everywhere active in the community, bequeathing to it the gift of the Sacred Scriptures and right understanding of them, equipping all of its members to be able to say from the depths of their being, "Jesus is Lord!" The Spirit likewise bequeaths life to the sacramental forms left to the community by the Lord. The Spirit completely fills the rites the community celebrates with the power of the Lord's hour. What Jesus began in the particular hour of his mounting the cross on Calvary, the Spirit renders present in all its force and glory in every time and space.

We see then that the event of the Paschal Mystery converges with the liturgical celebration of the sacraments. The rites that the community celebrates flow from the event itself. By entering into the rites the community enters into the very event. This is a way of speaking about liturgy that is applicable to any and all of the liturgies that the church celebrates. But our particular focus here will be to uncover these dimensions in the various liturgical celebrations that make up the Paschal Triduum and the fifty days of the Paschal season into which the Triduum opens. These celebrations are, of course, primarily celebrations of Eucharist and baptism; but especially during the Triduum these sacramental rites are celebrated in a unique way and stretched out in their component elements over several nights and days in such a way that their relation to the Paschal Mystery is revealed in all its wonder and splendor.

I have referred here a number of times to *rites* celebrated by the community. It is worth pausing a moment to be sure we understand this word, or better, understand what in fact is accomplished by means of rites or rituals. If I have insisted that the primordial significance of Christian rituals lies in the fact that the community receives them from the Lord himself, it is still necessary for us to realize that the Lord has given us something quite natural to human living and acting. Religious ritual is a part of every human community's way of enacting its communion with the divine sphere. So, although the particular rites of the Christian community are unique to it in what they ultimately intend and accomplish, the fact of celebrating rituals is not. This means that what we know about ritual in general can be helpful to us in understanding what is particular to our Christian rites.

First of all, let us be clear about all that is included in the term. By *rites* we mean all the component elements that make up the celebration in the concrete, material realm. This begins with the very place of gathering and with those who gather to celebrate. Place and the people gathered there are already part of the rite, as are the hour and day of the gathering, which are never without significance. Then the rites include all the ways of moving and speaking and singing and being silent that the assembly and various of its members will enact. It includes as well the taking up of particular symbols: bread, wine, oil, wood, water, wax, fire, clothing, touch, darkness, and light.

In the particular chapters of this book on particular liturgies we shall be speaking about the significance of all of these elements, and we will see how the particular way in which we combine them and move within them accomplishes nothing less than our own entering into the event of the Paschal Mystery. We are aiming at the "good grasp of [the liturgy] through the rites and prayers" that Vatican II's *Sacrosanctum Concilium* 48 urged as the means of the active participation of all the faithful in the liturgy.

Here is something more about rituals. Starting with St. Paul, the Christian community's use of the word *mystery* circled around the realities that are unique to that community's experience of God in the death and resurrection of Jesus. For St. Paul the central mystery is the cross of Christ (see 1 Cor 2:7). But why does he call the cross a *mystery*? He does so to express that something was hidden in the cross which we cannot understand without its being revealed. (See also Eph 1:9-10; 3:4-6; and Col 2:2-3.) Although St. Paul does not put it quite the way I am about to put it, I think the following is a fair way of summarizing the huge world of thought that swirls around his use of the word *mystery*. This summary gets us some way toward understanding how the same word came to be used for baptism and Eucharist. We could say that a *mystery* is a concrete something that when you bump into it puts you in contact with a divine reality. The cross is a concrete something; in it is hid the Lord of glory (1 Cor 2:7). The history of Israel is a concrete something; in it is the promise also for the Gentiles (Eph 3:4-6). Everything in heaven and on earth is a concrete something; it is all destined to be recapitulated in Christ (Eph 1:9-10; Col 2:2-3). Applying the same logic to baptism and Eucharist, we could say that being plunged into water and brought up again three times is a concrete something; in it is hidden a believer's dying and rising with Christ. The bread and wine of the Eucharist are concrete somethings; in them are hidden the very Body and Blood of Christ. All these rituals then are also called mysteries.

We are preparing to discuss in detail the rich and complex rituals of the Paschal Triduum and then of the whole paschal season culminating in Pentecost. These are mysteries. They are concrete somethings in which are hidden the death and resurrection of Christ and our communion in these. The Paschal Mystery itself is called *mystery* precisely because from the death of Christ all the rest that we have spoken about unfolds: his resurrection, ascension, sending of the Spirit, and establishing the church. During the Paschal Triduum and the paschal season we celebrate the mysteries which insert us into the Paschal Mystery.

Part 2

The Witness to Cross and Resurrection in the Lectionary and Liturgy from the Paschal Triduum to Pentecost

n this next part of our study, we carefully examine the liturgies of the Paschal Triduum and of the whole Easter season. We will pay close attention to the scriptural texts proclaimed within these liturgies, as well as to the particular rituals enacted in the course of them. We will see how the very celebration of these holy days has inserted every subsequent generation of believers from the apostles down to ourselves into the new life that unendingly flows forth from the risen body of the crucified Jesus. We will speak of the liturgy in a way that attempts to show how its celebration is meant to be for us immediate and effective contact with all that the Scriptures proclaim, with the entire synthetic vision of the reality expressed in the theological tradition. This is different from how the scriptural texts about resurrection are often treated, concentrating on what the text would have meant for its original audience. While not ignoring that kind of approach, my focus here will be to probe the particular liturgy in which a scriptural passage is proclaimed as a context in which the range and meaning of the text expand and become actual for us. So we take up the texts not in the neat order of, say, first Matthew, then Mark, then Luke, then John. Instead we take the scriptural texts as the liturgy presents them to us and try to understand why the liturgy uses them in this way. I call this *liturgical exegesis*. This will mean that we encounter texts of the Old Testament along with those of the New Testament as part of our examination of resurrection, for the liturgy itself uses these texts too for our encounter with the mystery.

We will see that the basic content of every liturgical celebration is the Paschal Mystery. By means of every liturgy celebrated, we enter into communion with that reality, with what I called on the first page of this book the most important event that has ever happened anywhere in the created universe.

The Scriptures narrate for us and give us theological categories for understanding the events of Jesus' death and resurrection, which are decidedly rooted in the past. By means of the liturgy we come into effective contact with those events and come to experience that they are not confined to the past. Indeed, resurrection means precisely that. Resurrection means that in Jesus the limits of death, space, and time are burst open and that what he did in one time and place is made available in every time and place to those who believe and put their trust in him. In the liturgy, the Jesus who *was* shows himself also to be a Jesus who *is*. In the liturgy, the Jesus who was crucified under Pontius Pilate reveals himself as gloriously alive and present to believers here and now. He shares his new life with those who believe in him.

The Triduum is prepared for by the forty days of Lent, and it opens up into the fifty days of Easter. So we will pause now at length on the Triduum, but our efforts will also extend into an examination of the entire paschal season with its climax in the solemnity of Pentecost. Pentecost is a climax, a lavish outpouring, a reaching of the point at which God cannot have given more, a point of arrival. And yet it is also a point of departure, the beginning of "the last days" and the birth of the church, that is, a whole new way of being in the world.

Six chapters organize the material in this part of the book, chapters that treat in sequence, Holy Thursday, Good Friday, the Paschal Vigil, Easter day and its Octave, Ascension, and Pentecost. A reader could perhaps follow these chapters with greater profit by having a Lectionary and/or Missal at hand. I will be citing texts, prayers, even rubrics from these. In fact, all these are the objects of our study.

Chapter 5

Holy Thursday:
Mass of the Lord's Supper

The Triduum begins with the Mass of the Lord's Supper. It is the simplest and most familiar to us of the Triduum liturgies because in effect it is a regular celebration of the Mass, with the addition of a foot-washing rite after the homily and a procession with the Blessed Sacrament at the end of the Mass. But if it is Mass as normal—admittedly an odd expression because Mass can hardly be normal—nonetheless everything about the celebration pulses with a quiet energy and joy unique to this day. This is because we know that, symbolically speaking, we are gathering on the very day and in the very hour when Jesus instituted the Eucharist. The Holy Spirit silently gives the assembly a peaceful determination to celebrate this mystery well, with reverence and with gratitude. We know that we are initiating the three days of liturgy that begin now with the memory of the Lord's Last Supper. We sense, with the Spirit's help, that we are every bit as much swept up into this event as were the original historical actors whose stories and words we shall hear.

This liturgy always begins in the late afternoon or evening. Gathering at this hour on this day, we know that we are gathered for the same reason that the disciples gathered with Jesus for a supper on the night before he died. We gather to receive from him what they received: his body and blood. But that is not to say enough. We receive his Body and Blood under the signs of bread and wine as a gift with which we are meant to discern the meaning of his death on the next day. So, just as happened in the original supper, in the eucharistic supper that we are about to celebrate, we will seek to connect all the signs of the meal to Jesus' death on the cross, an event whose force is imminent and which impinges more and more on the mood of the supper. As the hours of this evening advance, the day and hour of the cross come closer and closer.

The liturgy gets underway, however, in a space of unexpected light and joy. After many weeks of only the violet vestments with which the church signals its Lenten season of penance, white clothes and vestments adorn the priest and other ministers. The Missal even directs that the altar should be discreetly adorned with flowers, which would be striking since these have been lacking for so long during the Lenten season. The hour of gathering is unusual, and perhaps the setting sun is causing us to see our church building with a quality of light we don't usually experience there. The flowers, the white vestments, the evening light, a large assembly poised for the beginning of the Triduum—Christ invisibly penetrates this visible space and warms it with his presence. Whether or not we recall his words, Christ's heart, as he looks at this assembly and invades it, is surely filled with the sentiments he expressed when he said to his disciples at the beginning of the supper, "I have eagerly desired to eat this Passover [Pasch] with you before I suffer" (Luke 22:15).

The Entrance and the Gloria

In this atmosphere, with its palpable sense of expectation, the entrance antiphon is magnificent. In just a few lines it sings not only of the mystery of this particular liturgy but somehow captures from the very beginning the sense of all that will unfold in the coming days. The assembly sings the words of St. Paul from the Letter to the Galatians: "We should glory in the Cross of our Lord Jesus Christ" (Gal 6:14). This sets the tone from the start. This liturgy and all the liturgies will have the cross as their center, but not a cross before which we moan and groan; rather, the cross in which we glory. The antiphon continues, ". . . in whom is our salvation, life and resurrection." The tension, the mysterious balance, the inextricable blending of cross and resurrection which we spoke about in the opening chapters find here their first explicit verbal expression. In these days we will solemnly remember the death of Jesus on the cross. In this evening's liturgy, the signs of the meal will all point to the cross. In this cross, we sing, is our salvation, our life, and our resurrection. The last line of the song is jubilant: "through whom we are saved and delivered."

While this is being sung, the priest and the other ministers enter the church, and the priest incenses the altar, circling round it as he swings the censer. His moves mark the center of the action, the place where all that happens tonight will find its climax: the altar, the place of the cross which is our salvation, life and resurrection. Once all are gathered in their places, the priest greets the assembly and urges all to pray for mercy that we may celebrate these mysteries well. Yet no sooner is this done than the assembly bursts into a song it knows well but has not heard since the beginning of Lent: the Gloria. We are singing it strongly because we feel it has too long lain silent, and indeed, all the bells of the church ring while we are singing it. Even though we know that by this time tomorrow a much more sober tone will have overtaken us, still we cannot help this outburst of joy as we begin the Triduum. Christ is giving us his Body and Blood! With this gift we can walk through any darkness, any night, knowing that we shall arrive at resurrection life. Singing the familiar Gloria on this night, we are perhaps especially struck by some of its lines: Jesus Christ addressed as "Lamb of God" who "take[s] away the sins of the world." The image of Lamb will come often to the fore in the rest of this night and in the coming days.

A Reading from the Book of Exodus

All this excitement of the beginning is then calmed and collected, as it were, into an opening prayer whose language is replete with theological allusions. After this, the assembly is seated—being seated is also a liturgical posture, meaning we are ready to listen—and in solemn fashion a passage from Exodus 12 is proclaimed. This is the first of many passages of the Scripture to be read during the Triduum, and this beginning is of fundamental importance. It unveils the meaning not only of this day's liturgy but that of all the days to come. In the reading it is the Lord himself who speaks, and the divine oracle is introduced with the phrase, "The LORD said to Moses and Aaron in the land of Egypt." There follow the Lord's own instructions declaring the Pasch and how it shall be celebrated. We saw in chapter 2 that Exodus 12 was of enormous influence on the Christian understanding of Jesus' death and resurrection. The church rightly still uses this passage from Scripture to launch its celebration of the Paschal Triduum.

As we listen, we are mindful that, through the reader's voice, it is God's own voice that we hear in the midst of our assembly. The very words once spoken to Moses and Aaron in the land of Egypt are still sounding today, sounding in our community and declaring a Pasch in which we are about to share. It is wonderful to realize that what we are doing in our church this evening is in continuity with the same divine deed that God began with Moses and Aaron in Egypt. But as we already saw, that first historical Passover in Egypt with Moses and Aaron turns out to be but a prophecy of a greater and more definitive Passover: that of Jesus from death to resurrection. So, although we hear the Lord's words uttered at the first historical Passover, their meaning is referred in our believing minds to Jesus' Passover. In the same way that generations of Jewish believers heard these words and knew during the feast that all the saving power of the original event was made present to them in their celebration of the feast, so Christians hear these same words on this night and realize that all the saving power of Jesus' Passover is made available to them in this celebration.

How did Jesus enter into his Pasch? He did so by celebrating with his disciples the meal that is prescribed in this first reading. But during the course of the meal he quite consciously began to play some of its most fundamental themes in a new key, in the key of the new Pasch that he was about to accomplish. The food and drink of this meal were the language with which the story of Israel's Passover was told. Jesus draws on all its images now and intentionally summarizes or recapitulates all of Israel's history in himself. In the signs of the meal which he selects, he is conscious that he holds all of Israel and all her history in his hands as he takes up bread and wine, and he identifies that whole history with himself and with the death he will undergo on the morrow, saying over it, "This is my body, this is my blood."

It is impossible for our Christian minds not to think of all this as we listen to the reading from the book of Exodus. Its every word and image point to what Christ himself pointed to inside this same meal the night before he died. Its every word and image point to his life-giving death. It is into his definitive Pasch that we enter now by means of the same words. Let us see how those words from the historical exodus find their definitive meaning in Jesus' paschal meal, the same meal we are celebrating now.

"[E]very one of your families must procure for itself a lamb," says the Lord. "If a family is too small for a whole lamb, it shall join the nearest household in procuring one." By this liturgy we have done the same: we are many but have procured a single lamb, that is, Jesus, the Lamb of God. He is mysteriously "[t]he lamb [that is] a year-old male and without blemish." Then we hear that "[the lamb] shall be slaughtered during the evening twilight." When we hear those words, we understand that we are the assembly gathered in the evening twilight. Now Jesus the Lamb lets himself be slaughtered as he hands over his Body and Blood to us. "They shall take some of [the lamb's] blood and apply it to the two doorposts and the lintel of every house . . . That same night they shall eat its roasted flesh." We enact these prescriptions as we take the blood of Jesus in the cup he gives us. We "apply it" to our house by drinking it. We eat the flesh of the Lamb as we receive his Body given to us as food.

We are given instructions on how to eat: "with your loins girt, sandals on your feet and your staff in hand, you shall eat like those who are in flight." Our sharing in the banquet of Jesus' Body and Blood is not some cheerful sitting down to a party of like-minded friends who have no worries or troubles. No, we receive the Lamb's flesh and are protected by his blood while an enemy pursues us and is close on our heels. And it is precisely at this point in the reading that the Lord himself names the feast. He says, "It is the Passover of the LORD. For on this same night I will go through Egypt, striking down every firstborn of the land . . ." and then he adds, "[b]ut the blood will mark the houses where you are. Seeing the blood, I will pass over you" (Exod 12:11-13). Christians live in the world as those in flight. But the Lord himself is fighting for us, to strike down our enemies—which are sin and death—and we are protected through the blood of the Lamb.

A final injunction concludes the reading: "This day shall be a memorial feast for you, which all your generations shall celebrate with pilgrimage to the LORD, as a perpetual institution." Faithfulness to this injunction brings every subsequent generation of Christians into communion with Jesus' Pasch. That is what we are doing as we begin this year's Triduum. The Triduum is a "memorial feast" established by the Lord. It is a "perpetual institution."

The Responsorial Psalm

The proclamation of this passage from the book of Exodus should strike the gathered assembly with tremendous force. The Triduum has begun! God is acting here and now as he once acted of old. It is the Passover of the Lord! And so the assembly must sing the joy it feels in this moment, joy in its anticipation of a rich liturgy which has only just begun. For the refrain of our song, we use words of St. Paul, where we sing of the cup of the meal: "Our blessing-cup is a communion with the Blood of Christ." This orientates our interpretation of verses from Psalm 116 which follow.

The inspired words of the psalms give shape to our prayer. The words are peaceful, but they are no cheap or easy-got peace. "How shall I make a return to the LORD / for all the good he has done for me?" we sing. And, of course, we are thinking not just of stray favors for which we ought to be grateful; we are thinking mainly of the good the Lord has done for us in providing us with the Pasch. We continue, "The cup of salvation I will take up, / and I will call upon the name of the LORD." We think immediately of the joy of a banquet, and we are eager in anticipation of the cup of his blood that Jesus is soon to hand over to us in the course of the eucharistic celebration. The refrain is interspersed, and we repeat: "Our blessing-cup is a communion with the Blood of Christ." But as we dwell on this image, we also think of the cup that Jesus himself will take up in the course of this night, while he prays in agony in the garden that his cup of suffering might be taken from him but then adds, "Father . . . not my will but yours be done" (Luke 22:42; see also Matt 26:42; Mark 14:36; John 12:27). So it is Jesus who takes up the cup of salvation and calls upon the name of his Father. Jesus himself learned from this psalm that "Precious in the eyes of the LORD / is the death of his faithful ones," and he enters into the hour of his suffering with trust as he sings to his Father of what is about to happen: "To you I will offer sacrifice of thanksgiving / . . . . My vows to the LORD I will pay / in the presence of all his people." He is speaking of his death on the next day, which will not take place in obscurity but "in the presence of all his people." And in this liturgy we are singing his words with him. We share in his song, his cup, his sacrifice, his death.

A Reading from the First Letter of Paul to the Corinthians

The second reading, from St. Paul's First Letter to the Corinthians, is brief but very strong. It is several verses from a longer discussion of the Eucharist in this letter. In the verses we hear, St. Paul simply narrates what Jesus did at the supper "on the night he was handed over." He introduces his account of what he tells by reminding the Corinthian community that their knowledge of this sacred meal is a question of tradition, that is, that Paul received the account of the meal from the Lord himself and he handed it on to them. This faithful handing on of what Jesus did has continued through the generations to the present moment of our own celebration. We feel the presence of Paul in our own assembly. His words are for us still the authoritative apostolic witness of what Jesus did. The words of Jesus over the bread and over the cup are repeated: "This is my body . . . This cup is the new covenant in my blood." And with both bread and cup, Paul repeats the Lord's command: "Do this . . . in remembrance of me."

These words of the apostle handing on to us the words of the Lord most certainly define the present moment of our liturgy. On this night we are faithful to the Lord's command to do this meal in memory of him. And then St. Paul adds a very important comment of his own which interprets at depth what happens when the community fulfills the Lord's injunction and celebrates as he commanded. He says, "For as often as you eat this bread and drink the cup, you proclaim the death of the Lord until he comes"! These words have guided the church's understanding of the Eucharist from Paul's time to the present. They show us with unmistakable clarity that the Eucharist is a memorial of the Lord's death. But Paul uses a very strong verb. He says we *proclaim* the Lord's death. That is, his death is announced as something unexpectedly glorious. In this way his resurrection is made known—not explicitly, but by proclaiming his glorious death, the death of one whose coming again we await. Indeed, then, that is the "space" where Eucharist is celebrated by the church: in the space *between* the proclamation of his death and his coming again in glory. We are in that space now and respond "Thanks be to God" to our hearing the apostle's words. We understand that by means of our eucharistic celebration on this night, we enter into the space of the Triduum, a memorial of the Lord's death. By proclaiming his death this night and in the coming days, we shall come to know his resurrection.

A Reading from the Gospel according to John

It is perhaps surprising that one of the narrations of the institution of the Eucharist is not read as this liturgy's gospel reading. But as we have just noted, that account is supplied us already in the reading from 1 Corinthians. Instead, we read from the Gospel of John, the only one of the four gospels that does not have an account of the Last Supper eucharistic institution. But it is also the only gospel that does tell of the striking action of Jesus during that supper—namely, his rising from table to wash the disciples' feet. In John's gospel this passage marks a turning point from the first half of the story to the second. In the first half Jesus works a number of signs, each of which is followed by a discourse which debates its meaning. He cures a paralytic on the Sabbath; he cures a man born blind; he raises Lazarus from the dead. In the debates around these mighty deeds, those who believe in Jesus are increasingly distinguished from those who do not. Now, at this turning point in the gospel, Jesus is intimately involved in deep teaching with his disciples, with those who believe in him. He is preparing them for his ultimate sign, his ultimate mighty deed: his being lifted up on the cross. The gospel read in our assembly is meant to serve the same purpose. This year's Triduum is meant to be the same turning point in our lives.

This gospel passage (John 13:1-15) only increases the intensity of what we have already experienced in the first two readings. It too is not only an account of past events but also a description of the present moment and of the precise way in which Jesus is present to us now. In this first Liturgy of the Word during the Triduum, we still have a sense of the whole Triduum opening up to us by means of the inspired texts that are read. Every line of this gospel will help us to enter deeply into the meaning of the entire Triduum. The first sentence locates the scene in the context of Passover and then solemnly declares, "Jesus knew that his hour had come to pass from this world to the Father." All that is about to happen here is called Jesus' "hour." This expression is found frequently in John's gospel in the mouth of Jesus, and it indicates precisely that unique period of time in which Jesus accomplishes his saving deed: his death for us, his resurrection, and his ascension to his Father—all described here as "his hour . . . to pass from this world to the Father." The Triduum is, in fact, this hour, and this first line of the gospel is the solemn declaration that that hour has come. It has come for our community, here and now.

Love is the meaning of this hour. The evangelist says so with utter clarity and simplicity: "He loved his own in the world and he loved them to the end." Love is what Jesus will express in the washing of his disciples' feet, but what he does here first in symbolic gesture he will later do in actual fact. Jesus' death will be his ultimate expression of love, here described as his loving them "to the end," that is, loving them completely, to the end of his life, by the giving of his life. Love and death stand side by side here in the terrible drama that is about to unfold, and the sweet sentence about love is immediately followed by the ominous declaration, "The devil had already induced Judas, son of Simon the Iscariot, to hand him over." But then just as quickly the next sentence reveals a Jesus completely in charge of the scene. It begins, "So, during supper, fully aware that the Father had put everything into his power and that he had come from God and was returning to God . . ." What Jesus is about to do here he does with full awareness of the authority and mission entrusted to him by his Father, and he does it with awareness that this is his special Pasch, his having come from God and his returning to God. The sovereign calm with which Jesus steps into his hour reminds us of his extremely forceful words during his ministry: "No one takes [my life] from me, but I lay it down on my own. I have power to lay it down, and power to take it up again. This command I have received from my Father" (John 10:18). Judas who will betray him, soldiers who will arrest him, his own people who will hand him over to the Romans, those who will be charged with crucifying him—none of these takes Jesus' life from him. He freely lays it down. And so even though right here and now he finds himself in the dark atmosphere of Judas's decision to betray him, Jesus rises from the table and takes off his outer garment.

We see how carefully the evangelist has brought us to this moment of Jesus' unexpected action. It is Passover; it is his hour; it is love to the end; it is the devil's inducement of Judas's betrayal; it is Jesus' full awareness of his going to God. Now what Jesus does is presented by the evangelist as if in slow motion, for there are seven verbs, one after the other, and it is clear that the gospel writer wishes us to contemplate and ponder Jesus' every gesture. We are told that Jesus *rose* from the supper, *took off* his garments, *took* a towel and *tied* it round his waist. Then he *poured* water into a basin and began to *wash* his disciples' feet and *dry* them with the towel around his waist. What we contemplate in these carefully delineated moves is a symbolic enactment of the death that Jesus is about to undergo on the morrow. It is another version of the symbolic enactment that we have already seen in his actions around the bread and wine, in which he likewise referred by use of signs to the meaning of his impending death. Every one of the seven verbs can be understood on a first level to describe in a literal way the action that Jesus performs, but they are used in such a way that they simultaneously describe dimensions of the powerful and mysterious hour into which he is entering.

We read that he *rose* from the supper. It is not too early to hear, already now at the beginning of the Triduum, a hint of the glorious word *resurrection*. Jesus *rises* in the very midst of Judas's dreadful scheme. (In Greek this is the same verb that is used in descriptions of Jesus' resurrection. See, for example, 1 Cor 15:42-44.) No one takes his life from him. He has the "power to lay it down, and power to take it up again" (John 10:18, as above). Having risen from the supper, Jesus *takes off* his outer garment. We could say more literally, trying to translate very closely to detect the other levels of meaning, that he *lay down* his outer garment, in the same way that the Good Shepherd lays down his life for his sheep. (Again in Greek the verbs are the same. See John 10:11, 15, 17, 18.) Next, Jesus *takes* a towel and *ties* it round his waist. This is what Jesus will do with his cross: he takes it up and binds it round himself. Here the symbolic move shows that Jesus' cross is a profound kind of service for us. In his dying the "Teacher and Master" deliberately takes up and binds round himself the instruments that will cleanse us. Next we read that he *poured* water into a basin. How can we—who know already where this whole story is going—not see here an image of the blood that he will pour out for us on the cross? Then he begins to *wash* his disciples' feet. And here we have an image of the purpose of the blood he pours out. It means to be a cleansing for us. What by rights we ought to do for ourselves—if we could—is instead done for us by another. Having washed the disciples' feet, he *dries* them. Ah, how thorough is the Master in his service for us! He humbly employs the same sign of love that was directed toward him by the women who had poured ointment on his feet and dried them with their hair. (Compare John 11:2; 12:3; Luke 7:44.) In the same way that the evangelist stretches out these verbs for us to contemplate slowly the action of Jesus, we must imagine the minutes that pass over each of the disciples' feet as Jesus slowly washes them and dries them. He humbly handles their bodies with his own. He is expressing his love for them "to the end." They are amazed by his careful touch, and they are struck silent.

That is, all but Peter! Peter makes bold to object to what the Master is doing, and we would perhaps not be wrong to think that Peter says here what at least some of the others did not have the nerve to say. It was unheard of in Jewish custom that even a slave should be made to wash his master's feet. Peter, therefore, cannot accept what the group's "Teacher and Master" is doing for him and the others, even if he surely does realize that some symbolic gesture is being enacted. Whatever its meaning, he cannot bring himself to accept it.

This is not the first time Peter has had such a problem, and if we compare it to another important occasion, we see how crucial is the issue that Peter fails to grasp. (Of course, he is representative of us all in this failure.) During his ministry, Jesus carefully introduced to his small group of disciples his prediction of his suffering and death and subsequent resurrection on the third day. They probably understood little if anything of what he was saying. But Peter was not silent before this puzzle. He confidently corrected his teacher, and said, "God forbid, Lord! No such thing shall ever happen to you." (It is a similar way of saying, "You will never wash my feet.") At this first objection by Peter to his passion, Jesus firmly rebuked him, saying, "Get behind me, Satan! . . . You are not thinking as God does, but as human beings do." (See Matt 16:21-23.)

Now as he attempts to wash Peter's feet, the rebuke is just as strong. Peter's refusal of Jesus' symbolic action is nothing less than a refusal of Jesus' death for his sake. But Jesus is determined that he should serve Peter in this way, and so says, "Unless I wash you, you will have no inheritance with me." This corresponds to "Get behind me, Satan!" The suffering and cross that Jesus is about to undergo is God's way of thinking, not that of human beings.

Hearing this gospel at the beginning of our Triduum celebration is meant to be instructive for us all. In the atmosphere of the Last Supper which pervades the present moment of our celebration, Jesus reminds us with utter clarity of the attitudes necessary to enter with him into his hour. We have now arrived at the moment that he had predicted: Jesus must suffer greatly, be put to death, and raised again on the third day. All of us, like Peter, must yield to the incomprehensible and completely unexpected form of this "service," or we will have no inheritance with Jesus.

At the end of his symbolic action, Jesus reclines again with his disciples at table and offers an instruction on what he has just done. Understanding the symbolic action to indicate his death, we would be right then to understand what he next says as referring to that death for our sake. He says, "If I, therefore, the master and teacher, have washed your feet, you ought to wash one another's feet." He is saying much more here than that we should literally wash one another's feet. As this evening's conversation unfolds—chapters 13 through 17 of John's gospel all fall in the context of the Last Supper—Jesus will say the same directly: "Love one another as I love you," and then, "No one has greater love than this, to lay down one's life for one's friends" (John 15:12-13). The commandment for us is clear, and the apostle John draws the unmistakable conclusion for us in his first letter: "The way we came to know love was that he laid down his life for us; so we ought to lay down our lives for our brothers" (1 John 3:16).

The Washing of Feet

After the homily, what the apostle enjoins is now symbolically enacted in the next part of the liturgy. Jesus has said, "[Y]ou ought to wash one another's feet," and the apostle interprets, "we ought to lay down our lives for our brothers." So, the priest *rises* from his chair, *takes off* his outer garment, *ties* a towel round himself, and begins to *pour* water over the feet of twelve people selected from the congregation and to *dry* them. Meanwhile the choir and congregation are singing the words of the gospel we have just heard and meditated upon, the words which describe the Lord's actions, the words which express his dialogue with Peter. Those same words cover now the action of the bishop or priest. The congregation sings and watches. While the feet are being washed, a quiet and very firm sense of the presence of Christ in our midst invades the assembly.

There is always a bit of commotion involved, usually some difficulty in getting it all done smoothly. In fact, it is not meant to be easily done. The priest is down on the floor, and the community feels some shock in seeing him in this position. Those having their feet washed perhaps feel some embarrassment, some hesitation. Perhaps some who are watching from the congregation must struggle to check thoughts in themselves that they are not pleased to see the feet washed of someone known by them to be a not entirely upright person. Such shock and embarrassment and discomfort are a blessing for the community, a revelation. The action renders vivid what must always be a major dimension of the priestly ministry in the community—namely, that the priest is an icon of Christ at the head of the community, but precisely as head he is present as one who serves. He does not hesitate to wash the feet of the members of his flock, even the feet of one who shortly after may betray him.

The washing of the feet is a symbolic action, of course. But the enactment of this unsettling ritual in the midst of a particular community is always a renewal for that community of the grace of the priestly ministry and the bonds of love this is meant to build among all the members of the community. What Jesus did symbolically in the washing of the feet, he does the next day in very fact by laying down his life for his sheep. What the priest does symbolically he must also do in very fact in his service of the community. Every day he is meant to lay down his life for his sheep. And if the "teacher and master" does this, so ought we all to do. "I have given you a model to follow," says Jesus, "so that as I have done for you, you should also do." It is no wonder that next, as the gifts are prepared and brought to the altar, one of the traditional songs that is so gladly sung at this point proclaims, "Where charity and love prevail, there love is ever found. Brought here together by Christ's love, by love are we thus bound."

The Liturgy of the Eucharist

At the beginning of this chapter we suggested that everything about the celebration pulses with a quiet energy and joy unique to the day. Hopefully we have been able to detect some of that particular energy and joy in what we have reflected upon so far. Now we turn to what is the high point of this day's liturgy, the Liturgy of the Eucharist. It is celebrated no differently from how it is always done, but a definite atmosphere has been created by the proclamation of the particular texts of Scripture that we examined, by the washing of the feet, by the chants that have expressed the community's joy and wonder. In this atmosphere of our celebration, in the late afternoon or early evening, we are uniquely poised to enter with renewed depth into the eucharistic mystery. In fact, we can think of the content of the scriptural readings, the effect of the washing of the feet, and the evening hour as a unique door through which we enter the celebration of this day's Eucharist.

I feel tempted now to begin a commentary on the eucharistic prayer, but I will resist because this book's focus lies elsewhere, even if the eucharistic prayer contains it all in condensed form. (The reader may want to consult my *What Happens at Mass*,[1] where there is an ample commentary on the eucharistic prayer.) A few things, however, can be noted here. I want at least to give a nod to the preface that is peculiar to this day, for it is by means of this text that we enter into the rest of the eucharistic prayer that we use also at other celebrations of the Eucharist. This preface is thick with theological content. It will be too rich to absorb if we are not especially attentive.

We should note that in it Christ is specified as "true and eternal Priest." The word *priest* shifts us to yet a deeper level of all that has been said heretofore of Jesus in this liturgy. A priest offers sacrifice. That word is applied to what Jesus does during the course of the supper as an interpretative key for us.

Jesus the priest is said to have "instituted the pattern [in Latin, *forma*] of an everlasting sacrifice." The "form" is what Jesus does in this supper together with his asking us to repeat it in his memory. It is a tremendous word. The meal is a *form*; the footwashing is a *form*; it points to the *form* of his self-emptying death. And the liturgy we now celebrate is in this same *form*. Jesus institutes this *form* as an everlasting *form* that we are to repeat. Consequently, in the final part of the preface a huge "and so" comes bursting forth from the lips of the priest who leads our prayer. *For this very reason*, it tells us, we want to sing glory to God by uniting our song "with the Angels and Archangels, with Throne and Dominations, and with all the hosts and powers of heaven." Their capacities of comprehending these mysteries far exceed ours, and how good it would be then if we could join our prayers with theirs. Together with them, we beg to be able to sing, "Holy, Holy, Holy Lord!"

After this, the eucharistic prayer continues as usual. Even so, as I already suggested, from the very beginning of this liturgy we have felt the specialness of celebrating the Eucharist on the very day and in the very hour when Jesus instituted this sacrament. That special sense reaches its climax now in all that is accomplished in the course of this prayer. For example, how could we fail to follow intently the words and actions of the priest as he recounts before the Father in the presence of the whole assembly what Jesus did with the bread and wine at the Last Supper? What Jesus was doing then he did

---

1. Jeremy Driscoll, *What Happens at Mass*, rev. ed. (Chicago: Liturgy Training Publications, 2011).

because "his hour had come." That hour never passes away. And by the priest's repeating the actions and words of Jesus, all of us enter into that very same hour.

We grasp that by means of our very celebration we, no less than the apostles at the Last Supper, are present with Jesus and are participants with him as he enters into the hour in which he is handed over for us. In that hour we receive from him, under the signs of bread and wine, his very Body and Blood. With this gift we are meant to understand the meaning of his death for us on the next day; with it we are meant to understand as well how he is still present to us after he rises from the dead. His command to repeat these signs in memory of him contains a divine plan that will be instructive for us, for as we have heard the apostle Paul say, "As often as you eat this bread and drink the cup, you proclaim the death of the Lord until he comes!" Our celebration of the Eucharist instructs us in the whole meaning of the Triduum, that is, in the whole meaning of the Lord's death and resurrection and our participation in them.

It is clear that in the intensity of this atmosphere our reception of the Lord's Body and Blood on this night requires our closest attention and deepest possible devotion. Of course, attention and devotion are appropriate every time we receive the Eucharist. But our reception on this night is meant to renew our fervor for all subsequent receptions. And, indeed, it does seem to work this way. In any case, that is what we hope for. The possibilities for deepening our devotion are further increased in the unusual way in which this particular celebration of the Mass finishes. We turn to that now.

The Transfer of the Most Blessed Sacrament

In most celebrations of the Mass, after the distribution of Communion, any remaining fragments of the Lord's Body are put in the tabernacle; his precious Blood is entirely consumed and the vessels cleansed. When the prayer after Communion has been said, the priest blesses the assembly in the name of the Trinity and dismisses it. At this Mass, however, something noticeably different happens to these various liturgical parts. In fact, many additional hosts have been consecrated at this Mass so that we can receive Communion tomorrow, on Good Friday, when no Mass is celebrated. Now a ciborium with these hosts is left on the altar and not placed in the tabernacle.

And rather than dismiss the assembly, the priest kneels before the Blessed Sacrament present on the altar and incenses it. Kneeling and incensing are both acts of adoration here. The church wants to enact her faith that Jesus, who is truly God and God's Son become flesh for us, is entirely present in the sacrament on the altar. As such then, in this sacrament (which has been given to us "today!") he can be worshipped and adored.

After the incensing and adoration, a procession is formed in which the Blessed Sacrament will be carried through the church. All the people take lighted candles and begin to sing, either joining in the procession itself, or, if this is not possible, following the procession with the eyes and the movement of their bodies. In any case, the Blessed Sacrament is carried as a precious and even fragile treasure might be borne along. The priest has wrapped round his shoulders a special veil, and with it he covers and seems to protect the gift he carries. A cross leads the procession, and someone with a smoking censor immediately precedes the priest. The procession passes through the whole body of the church. The passage is meant to bring the Blessed Sacrament close to all the people and to sanctify anew the spaces through which it passes. It is true that we have all just received this same sacrament, and the same divine presence that we honor with these external signs is likewise being carried in our own bodies and hearts. Even so, such a reverent procession enables us to take the measure of how great and holy is the one whom we have received and whose presence we bear within. We experience the Sacrament as something other than ourselves, however intimately we might be united to the Lord by means of it.

If the space or spaces of the community permit it, the Blessed Sacrament is carried to a place other than the main church itself in which the liturgy has just been celebrated. Or if this is not possible, some space within the church is arranged as a place of reposition where the Blessed Sacrament will be adored by some of the faithful from now until midnight and kept until it is distributed during the next day's liturgy. People are urged to stay, as their circumstances permit, in the space of this silent adoration or to return to it later during the course of the evening. The liturgy that has just been completed is a huge amount to absorb, and a period of silent prayer and adoration in the presence of the Blessed Sacrament is meant to help us absorb how very much has been done, indeed how very much has begun.

For the Paschal Triduum has begun. This, its first liturgy, has been *stunning* in the widest possible sense of that word. So will its other liturgies be, each in its own way. This is why the church urges us to spend time after the Mass of this day in further contemplation. The intensity of prayer on this night can renew us for prayer before the Blessed Sacrament all throughout the year.

Now it is time to turn to the liturgy of the next day, Good Friday. Its atmosphere will be very different from this, but not by way of some simple contrast. Rather, today's liturgy has prepared us—trained us up, as it were—to grasp all the riches of the Good Friday liturgy, just as Jesus gave us the Eucharist as an instrument for grasping how glorious and life-giving his death is. On Good Friday we shall be celebrating that glorious and life-giving death.

Chapter 6

Good Friday:
The Celebration of the Passion of the Lord

Reading the first words of instructions in the Roman Missal for Good Friday, one could be struck by the starkness of what is stated and the directions that are given. "In accord with very ancient tradition, on this and the following day the Church does not celebrate the Sacraments at all, except for Penance and the Anointing of the Sick . . . The altar should be completely bare: without a cross, without candles, without cloths." The liturgy that is about to unfold is different, then, from all others throughout the year. We will not be celebrating the Eucharist, and at no time during this day will other sacraments be celebrated, apart from those that tend to the pressing spiritual or physical needs of people (penance and anointing the sick). It is sad, even alarming, to see the altar looking so bare, bereft of its usual cloths and flaming candles, no cross to adorn it. The hour for this liturgy is also an unusual time for us to find ourselves in church. It is to take place around three o'clock in the afternoon, obviously because this is the hour at which the Lord breathed his last. (In places where that hour is not possible—perhaps because of work or other impediments—the liturgy can take place later.) Even before the ceremony begins, simply by looking around the church at this unexpected hour, we understand that we are gathered to a different purpose from the one that usually brings us together in this space. It should give us pause that the church does not celebrate the sacrament of the Eucharist on this day and the next. (The Vigil which begins on Saturday night is considered part of the liturgy of Sunday. We will speak of that when we come to it.) After all, is not the Eucharist a memorial of the Lord's death? So would not Good Friday, the very day of his death, be a most fitting day to celebrate the Eucharist?

To understand "this very ancient tradition" we must perhaps use our intuition, trying to feel an instinct that the church has had virtually from the very beginning, an instinct that on the day of the Lord's death and on the next day as he lies in the tomb, the church must abstain from all festivity and observe a severe fast, even a fast from the Eucharist itself. Such a fast sharpens our hunger for celebrating the Eucharist, which we will do next at the Paschal Vigil. But fasting on this day and abstaining from celebrating Mass also has the effect of creating a mood in the whole day. The force of the memory of the death of Jesus is so strong and vivid on this day that the memorial of his death that we normally celebrate in Mass is suspended, and the whole day itself—a day without Mass—functions as a kind of "sacrament" that puts us in touch in a different way with the unfathomable event of the death of the Son of God on the cross. All day long it is the day of Jesus' death. All day long its memory should fill our minds, our hearts, our hungry bodies.

Even so, what we are about to do in this liturgy is by no means a sort of funeral liturgy for Jesus. It is not a liturgy of mourning and lament. We do not have to pretend for a while that we do not know that Jesus is risen from the dead, thinking only for the next few days of his terrible death and burial. Indeed, the precise title for this liturgy in the Roman Missal is *"Celebration* of the Passion of the Lord." We are going to *celebrate* the Lord's Passion—obviously not as one celebrates some cheerful event. But it is *celebration* nonetheless, for, as we shall see in this very liturgy, the Lord's cross, the Lord's death, is victory and life. His death is a triumph, for by his dying he destroys death for us. And we who remember his death today do so precisely because we know him to be risen. The story of Jesus' death—celebrating it—is a necessary part of the announcement of resurrection. This is, as we said in part 1, Pasch as both passion and passage. Death and resurrection—it is not first one and then the other. They are always inextricably intertwined—in Jesus' Pasch, in our Christian lives, in the liturgies of the Triduum. In today's liturgy we carefully remember the death of Jesus, and doing so will be a magnificent revelation to us of the divine deed in which, yes, death and its horrors are all too real, and in which nonetheless that death is the glorious lifting up of the one who draws all things to himself.

Today's liturgy consists of three parts: the Liturgy of the Word, the Adoration of the Cross, and Holy Communion. In turn, each of these parts is made up of smaller units. I hope to comment on everything now, large and small. To help us follow all that is there, I will give titles to each of the smaller parts as they come, noting for the reader also when the liturgy shifts from one of its three major parts to another.

Entrance and Opening Prayer

We have already taken note of the stark atmosphere of the church, especially concerning the altar. We are gathered again at an hour that is unusual for us. (This fact subtly hints that the liturgies of yesterday and today are meant to speak to each other.) Now the way in which the priest and the other ministers enter the church for the beginning of the celebration will add greatly to this unfamiliar atmosphere. The priest and deacon are wearing red vestments, and it is clear enough why. They are draped in the blood of Christ. They enter in silence and go to the altar, while all the people stand. They make a reverence to the altar and then—surprising and dramatic gesture!—they prostrate themselves on the ground. The silence continues, and all the people fall to their knees, silent as well. All other liturgical gatherings in the year open with song and joyful procession. Today, by contrast, the silence is loud, and we see the priest and deacon lying on the ground before the altar.

What do these gestures mean—the prostration, the kneeling, the startling silence? It is important to understand them rightly. They are not principally intended as a sign of mourning or lament over the death of Jesus, though such a meaning is not precluded. Dramatic gestures performed in silence inevitably evoke a wide range of meanings, difficult to pin down with precision. So it is meant to be. But the principal sense of the wordless prostration and kneeling is that of profound adoration before the epiphany of God that is about to take place in this liturgy. In a way completely unimaginable to the human mind or heart that has searched for God through the millennia of the race's existence, God reveals himself now as holy, mighty, and immortal in the cross of Christ. In this liturgy God reveals what and who God is. In the presence of this unfathomable form of revelation, we begin by lying on our faces in silence before the all-holy God. We could use St. Paul's words in his First Letter to the Corinthians to describe the moment. He says, "We speak God's wisdom, mysterious, hidden . . . which none of the rulers of this age knew, for if they had known it, they would not have crucified the Lord of glory. . . . [T]his God has revealed this to us through the Spirit" (1 Cor 2:8-10). In this liturgy the crucified Jesus will be revealed to us as the Lord of Glory. This is today's mystery. This is the mystery we celebrate.

After this time of silent adoration—and its length should not be shortened, however discomforting it may be for some—the priest goes to the chair and, without one of the customary greetings of the people that usually opens a liturgy, without even the invitation to pray, he begins immediately the words of the opening prayer. This prayer slices the silence open with a clean thrust. Typical of the lean, understated style of so many of the prayers of the Roman Missal, this prayer comes immediately to the point. "Remember your mercies, O Lord," it begins. I call this "understated" because what in fact will be remembered in this liturgy is not merely some vague sense of general mercy directed toward human beings by an almighty God. No, it will be the abundant, infinite, concrete mercies that are offered to us precisely in the cross of Christ. None of this need be said; such thoughts have filled our minds in the silent adoration. Barely able to speak, we simply ask, "Remember your mercies, O Lord," knowing thereby that we are referring the Father to the cross of his Son.

Continuing in this sober tone, the prayer manages to formulate one further request. It asks, ". . . and with eternal protection sanctify your servants . . ." This is obviously a good thing to ask for, but the final phrase of the prayer dares to suggest to God why he ought to treat his "servants" in this way. It describes them as "your servants, for whom Christ your Son, by shedding his Blood, established the Paschal Mystery." A huge piece of theology is laid down in this short phrase. It perfectly expresses what we said about the Paschal Mystery in chapter 1, that *Pasch* and *paschal* do not simply mean Easter and resurrection. This prayer says that the shedding of Christ's blood on the cross is already the Paschal Mystery. It is Pasch as passion. God's Son shed his blood for us, the prayer says. If, in virtue of this blood, we ask for protection and that God sanctify us, the inspiration for these requests come from the blood of the Passover lamb, whose blood was spread over the houses of those celebrating so that they would be protected from the destroying angel who was to pass through Egypt on this very night.

I interrupted the prayer to comment on its various phrases. But let us now see it all at once, mindful now of how very much has been packed into this terse style of prayer. "Remember your mercies, O Lord, and with eternal protection sanctify your servants, for whom Christ your Son, by shedding his Blood, established the Paschal Mystery. Who lives and reigns for ever and ever. Amen." With words like these the church dares to break the holy silence with which the liturgy began.

If, though, the silence has been broken, so careful is this prayer that it is possible to say also "just barely broken." With this all but silent beginning completed, the first of the three parts of the liturgy now gets under way. It is a Liturgy of the Word, whose various parts shall be treated now each in turn.

A Reading from the Book of the Prophet Isaiah

The first reading from the book of the prophet Isaiah emerges from the barely broken silence like a trumpet blast. At first the prophet speaks in God's own voice. The assembly is well aware of the reason for today's gathering. We are met to remember the death of Jesus. That is the scene, that is the event, in all our minds. Yesterday's liturgy already inserted us into that "hour." We are kept in it now and made to enter more deeply into its mystery by the very words of God. The words function as a kind of commentary from God's point of view on Jesus hanging on the cross. We are immediately invited to perceive the glory hidden in the cross. God says of his Son, "See, my servant shall prosper, / he shall be raised high and greatly exalted." Yes, Jesus is "raised high" on the cross, but we are to understand this as his being raised high in a great exaltation. Jesus already speaks like this in John's gospel of his being lifted up. He said, "And when I am lifted up from the earth, I will draw everyone to myself" (John 12:32). And again, "When you lift up the Son of Man, then you will realize that I AM" (John 8:28). Jesus is speaking of three senses of his being lifted up: on the cross, in resurrection, and in ascension to his Father. All this was already said through the divine oracle uttered by the prophet Isaiah: "See, my servant shall prosper, / he shall be raised high and greatly exalted."

The one raised high is described as the "servant" of God, so thoroughly is Jesus' accomplishing his Father's will as he is raised up.

And it is predicted that this servant shall prosper. His being raised up on the cross is but the beginning of that upward movement that will take him all the way to ascension to his Father, where there will be returned to him "all the glory that was his before the world began" (see John 17:5).

But after this bright beginning a contrast is introduced. Jesus, the servant who is to be exalted, is described in all the agony of his crucifixion. He is said to be one whose look was "marred . . . beyond human semblance / and his appearance beyond that of the sons of man." Jesus enters into human death in an appalling form, the cruel form of a capital execution. "The most handsome of men" as one of the psalms calls him (Ps 45:3), has now been "marred . . . beyond human semblance." The comment of God continues: "So shall he startle many nations, / because of him kings shall stand speechless." These words describe the history of the world from the time of Jesus' crucifixion even to our present. The story of the cross has startled nations, riveted their attention, and converted them. It has startled others and caused them to turn away. But in any case, because of the ultimate glory of the ignominious cross, the message of the cross has gone out to all the nations and startled them. This is as the divine words foretell: "for those who have not been told shall see, / those who have not heard shall ponder it."

If the cross startled and will continue to startle nations, we should not forget that in the present moment we now are among the nations, and so the prophetic words apply to our community and our culture as well. Not only that, but as the early desert monks used to interpret the word "nations" in the Scripture, there are "nations" within each person—that is, a host of energies and tendencies and traits, each of which must be converted to the Lord. "Praise the LORD, all you nations" (Ps 117:1) can mean the same as "all my being, bless his holy name" (Ps 103:1). And just as the marred appearance of Jesus on the cross shall startle nations, it also shall startle all that is within me. The "kings" within me should "stand speechless."

Each year on Good Friday when I hear this text proclaimed, I am amazed at the clarity and precision with which the prophetic words, pronounced some six centuries before the birth of Christ, find their fullest sense in the events surrounding the death of Jesus on the cross. Here we can immediately grasp the sense of that line we proclaim about the Holy Spirit in the Creed, where we say, "[The Spirit] has spoken through the prophets." Fewer texts could indicate this more clearly than this one from Isaiah that we read today. The very details of the Passion are present in what the prophet says. We can understand how natural it was for the early Christians to read texts of this kind and understand them as a foreshadowing of Christ.

In any case, in what follows it is no longer God's voice that is directly heard, but the prophet's. The prophet expresses the amazement of us all before the spectacle of Jesus' cross. He exclaims, "Who would believe what we have heard?" There follows a mysterious entwining of passion and passage, of suffering and glory. On the one hand, the depth of the suffering of Jesus is further described, but concomitant with that, a glory hidden within. We continue to be struck by how tightly the words fit the life and death of Jesus. "[T]here was in him no stately bearing . . . that would attract us to him. . . . He was . . . a man of suffering, accustomed to infirmity . . . spurned, and we held him in no esteem." And yet, the prophet claims, he is full of significance for us, a significance that concerns our very salvation. "Yet it was our infirmities that he bore, / our sufferings that he endured / . . . he was pierced for our offenses, / crushed for our sins; . . . / by his stripes we were healed."

Jesus' own interior attitude during his Passion is also foretold by the prophet. "Though he was harshly treated, he submitted / . . . like a lamb led to the slaughter / . . . he was silent and opened not his mouth . . ." Even the details of Jesus' burial are foreseen by the farseeing eye of the prophet: "[A] grave was assigned him among the wicked / and a burial place with evildoers, / though he had done no wrong / nor spoken any falsehood."

These are, as we have already heard, startling and amazing things. But in effect, resurrection is indirectly indicated as well in what the prophet pronounces: "If he gives his life as an offering for sin, / he shall see his descendants in a long life." We and all believers are those descendants, and his "long life" is the eternal life the Father gives him in raising him from the dead. And now the voice of the oracle changes again, and it is once more the Father's voice that is heard, continuing to proclaim the promise of resurrection: "Because of his affliction / he shall see the light in fullness of days / . . . Therefore I will give him his portion among the great, / and he shall divide the spoils with the mighty, / because he surrendered himself to death / . . . he shall take away the sins of many, / and win pardon for their offenses."

Thus ends the first reading. It is clear enough, I hope, why I described it as a trumpet blast. The tone is sounded for the rest of the perfectly balanced celebration that follows, the celebration that ponders and exults in the mysterious interweaving of cross and glory. The whole assembly responds with wonderment as it cries out after this blast, "Thanks be to God."

Throughout my commentary on this Old Testament reading, I have unhesitatingly referred all its words to Jesus and the hour of his death. In doing so, I am following the most ancient of apostolic traditions concerning this very passage. In the Acts of the Apostles, the wonderful story is told of an Ethiopian eunuch, a minister to the queen of the Ethiopians, as he travels along in great splendor, reading this very passage from Isaiah. The deacon Philip is sent by an angel to ride along beside this Ethiopian, and when Philip comes up alongside his chariot, he asks the Ethiopian if he understands the passage. He immediately poses a question to Philip. He asks, "About whom is the prophet saying this? About himself, or about someone else?" We hear in response this wonderful line: "Then Philip opened his mouth and, beginning with this scripture passage, he proclaimed Jesus to him" (Acts 8:26-40). In our community the same apostolic witness resounds in this Good Friday reading.

The Responsorial Psalm

The refrain of the responsorial psalm places the last words of Jesus, as reported in Luke's gospel, on the lips of the congregation: "Father, into your hands I commend my spirit" (Luke 23:46). In fact, Jesus' words are the words of a psalm (Ps 31:6), with the slight but significant addition of Jesus' intimate name for God: "Father." Interspersed then with this refrain are other verses of the psalm from which Jesus makes his prayer. As is so often the case of the psalms when they are prayed in Christian liturgy, this psalm is a revelation and a setting into motion in our midst of the intimate prayer of Jesus to his Father. It is often Christ Jesus himself who is praying in the person of the psalmist, and his words are directed to God the Father. In this psalm, prayed at this point in the Good Friday liturgy, there is revealed to us something of the way Jesus prayed to his Father during the long, drawn-out hours of his dying. The effect of the whole congregation singing the refrain at regular intervals as the cantor sings the individual verses of the psalm is to insert the very prayer of Jesus into the whole congregation. Jesus' prayer throughout his agony pulses through the whole community and becomes its prayer as well. In the singing rhythm and exchange between cantor and community, the community gradually begins to sense what it means to participate in the Passion of Christ. It involves not just our own suffering in life but also a way of praying, a way revealed in our singing now. Jesus' agony gathers our world to itself and commends it to the Father as the hour of his dying.

What we learn from the psalm verses, one by one, is the depth of Jesus' trust in his Father as he dies, even as the depths of his anguish are likewise revealed. These mysterious depths are shared with the congregation as it sings and listens. "In you, O LORD, I take refuge; / let me never be put to shame / . . . you will redeem me, O LORD, O faithful God." It is no vague sense of redemption that Jesus hopes for here. In this context the sense is quite concretely, "You will raise me up from the dead, O Lord, O faithful God." In the next verse we hear Jesus' prayer as he is mocked by those who surround his cross. "I am . . . a laughingstock to my neighbors / . . . I am forgotten like the unremembered dead." But even from the depths of such misery and desolation—to which our own is gathered—Jesus persists in his hope: "But my trust is in you, O LORD / . . . In your hands is my destiny; rescue me / from the clutches of my enemies and my persecutors." Jesus' persistence in hope is meant to become also our own. Again, the rescue for which he prays is no vague request; it is quite precisely a request to be raised up after death. This also is the sense of the tender plea that follows: "Let your face shine upon your servant; / save me in your kindness." The last words that the cantor sings—that *Jesus* sings!—are addressed not to the Father but to all of us who have been joined to his prayer in the hour of his agony. He urges, "Take courage and be stouthearted, / all you who hope in the Lord." And again, for the last time, the refrain: "Father, into your hands I commend my spirit." And are we not to think that Jesus' prayer will be answered by the Father in whom he trusts so much?

A Reading from the Letter to the Hebrews

The second reading (Heb 4:14-16; 5:7-9), like the first, is meant to help us penetrate the mystery of this day, the mystery of the cross.

Yet its approach to the question is considerably different from that of Isaiah. In fact, the whole of the Letter to the Hebrews is a profound theological meditation on Jesus' death and exaltation in glory. The author uses the categories of Jewish theological thought, as expressed in their Scriptures, to grasp the significance of Jesus' dying and exaltation. (Actually the word *resurrection* is never used in this letter. A range of other images is used, hovering around the sense of *exaltation*.) The reading combines two short portions of a much longer passage in which the movement from death to exaltation is considered as an exercise of priesthood by Christ. His shedding of his blood is in fact the priestly offering of a sacrifice. His exaltation at "the right hand of the Majesty on high" (Heb 1:3) is an entry into a heavenly sanctuary where with his sacrifice he perpetually intercedes before God on our behalf.

We are perhaps at least vaguely accustomed to such language to describe the death of Jesus, but it is worth our pausing to consider how deep is the insight achieved by the author of this letter when he describes it as a priestly act. In Jewish religion, or in fact in any religion, the offering of a sacrifice is a cultic act, a ritual. It is a symbolic enactment of a people's desire to offer themselves to a god and to establish themselves thereby in some sort of favorable relationship with the god. But Jesus' death on the cross is certainly no ritual, no symbolic enactment. His death is the cruel execution of a human being. The author of this letter knows all this. So when he uses the categories of priesthood and sacrifice to describe the death of Jesus, he achieves a tremendous theological insight. He is claiming that what all cultic sacrifices could only weakly point to and symbolically achieve is now in fact definitively achieved by Jesus, not in a cultic act, but quite literally in his dying and his being exalted at the right hand of the Father. This is a new and definitive sacrifice, a new and definitive priesthood.

The passage read in today's liturgy, selected from a much longer development of these themes, declaims, as it were, this priesthood. These are words that are meant to help us penetrate the deepest meaning of the cross. "Brothers and sisters," the announcement begins, "we have a great high priest who has passed through the heavens, Jesus, the Son of God . . ." What the eyes of our minds see is Jesus in his agony on the cross; what we are to understand is that here is a great high priest who is entering the heavenly sanctuary with the sacrifice of his own blood. And this priest is one of us. "[W]e do not have a high priest who is unable to sympathize with our weaknesses, but one who has similarly been tested in every way, yet without sin." Precisely from what he is suffering in the hour of his dying, Jesus is able to be a priest who sympathizes with us. As we gaze on this scene and discern its sense through these words, we are invited to approach the cross, not described as a place of execution but as ever so much more. "So let us confidently approach the throne of grace to receive mercy and to find grace for timely help." The cross: a throne, *the* throne of grace!

The next paragraph of the passage uses the category of the characteristic priestly act of intercession. Jesus' whole life of prayer, but especially his manner of prayer in the hour of his dying, of which we have had some glimpse in our meditation on the responsorial psalm, is this great priestly intercession. "In the days when Christ was in the flesh, he offered prayers and supplications with loud cries and tears to the one who was able to save him from death . . ." With these words we are meant to grasp the loud cry that Jesus emits before he breathes his last. He is praying to "the one who was able to save him from death . . ." "[A]nd," the passage continues, "he was heard because of his reverence." What is the "reverence" with which Jesus prays? It is his obedience to the Father's will, his "not my will but yours be done" that he prayed during his agony in the garden. "[H]e learned obedience from what he suffered," the author tells us. As the Father's inscrutable will has it, Jesus' suffering will take him all the way through to death, precisely to reveal that his obedience is total, his trust, total. This is why his loud cry "was heard." Mysteriously, the Father's saving Jesus from death does not save Jesus from dying. Rather, precisely because of the manner of his dying, God exalts him. This exaltation includes his being rendered a saving source for us. This is how the passage concludes: "and when he was made perfect, he became the source of eternal salvation for all who obey him." (We will discuss again the theological frameworks of Hebrews in considering an option for the second reading on the solemnity of the Ascension. See below, pp. 132–34.)

Perhaps it is useful to observe once again at the end of this second reading that the tone and sense of today's liturgy is by no means simply a mournful remembering of Jesus' death. We are not pretending, for the sake of dramatic effect on Easter, that we do not know that Jesus has been raised from the dead. No, we are remembering his death as triumph and glory. We are seeing him "made perfect"; we are encountering in the cross "the source of eternal salvation." "[W]e have a great high priest who has passed through the heavens"!

The Passion according to John

The first two readings and the responsorial psalm have been very forceful, but the real high point of the Liturgy of the Word on this day comes now with the gospel, the narrative of Jesus' passion and death as recounted by the evangelist John (John 18:1–19:42). John's account is chosen for this day because in it there shines forth—more than in Matthew, Mark, and Luke's accounts of the passion—all the glory that is hidden in Christ's passion. It clearly is "his hour . . . to pass from this world to the Father" (John 13:1). In fact, Jesus' prayer, "Father . . . give glory to your Son" (John 17:1), is already being mysteriously answered in the way the passion unfolds. Here, as throughout the rest of this gospel, in the particular way in which events are recounted and various things said by Jesus and others, there are always multiple levels of meaning to be discerned. On the literal level we can simply follow the events of Jesus' arrest, trial, crucifixion, and death. But by carefully attending to the language of the evangelist, we begin to discern also deeper dimensions of what is occurring. This would be true in just a private and prayerful reading and study of the text; it becomes even stronger when the text is proclaimed in liturgical celebration. In many places it is the custom to either read or sing the text, assigning different parts respectively to a narrator, to the voices of the various people who speak, including the crowd, and to the voice of Jesus himself. This sharpens the dramatic effect and causes the story being told really to become "event" for the community that listens carefully to the proclamation. The Holy Spirit, who inspired the evangelist, is now moving through the assembly opening the minds and hearts of the hearers to the deeper levels of meaning.

The passage is lengthy, and a good deal of its force comes from that fact. We cannot examine it in all its details here, but we can look at several representative moments or characteristics of the account that will help us to enter into its spirit. For example, the story opens with Jesus and his disciples in the garden. Judas is coming with a band of soldiers to arrest Jesus. The disciples seem unaware of their approach, but—note the evangelist's emphasis—"Jesus, knowing everything that was going to happen to him, went out and said to them . . ." That is, he does not hesitate for a moment; it does not occur to him to flee or hide. As we have often noted, no one takes Jesus' life from him. He has "power to lay it down, and power to take it up again" (John 10:18). Then Jesus says to the band of soldiers and guards, "Whom are you looking for?" They answer him, "Jesus the Nazorean." He says, "I AM." We are meant to understand this answer as saying something more than "I am the one you are looking for," though on the literal level it means at least that. But here Jesus pronounces as his own the divine name mysteriously revealed of old to Moses, "I am who am" (Exod 3:14). This explains why those around him all fell to the ground when he said it. Usually when someone about to be arrested says, "I'm the one you're looking for," it does not have this effect on those who would do the arresting. But the pronouncement of the divine name, by the one whose name it is, does have this effect. Jesus drives the point home. Speaking to them as they are on the ground, he asks again, "Whom are you looking for?" Again they answer, "Jesus the Nazorean." And again he pronounces the divine name, adding this time, "So if you are looking for me, let these men go." Here we see from the very beginning that Jesus intends to go to his death in our stead, in order that we may be let go. We remember another time when Jesus said, "I am": "I am the good shepherd. The good shepherd lays down his life for the sheep" (John 10:11). And everything that unfolds now will be the manifestation by Jesus of his divine name: I am who am.

Throughout all that happens, Jesus will walk with majesty, with power, with the air of someone who knows that he "had come from God and was returning to God" (John 13:3), as we heard said when Jesus began to wash his disciples' feet, the symbolic enactment of what is beginning to happen now. Brought before the high priest, Jesus hardly deigns to answer him, and when he does, he does so with authority. His tone earns him a sharp blow from one of the temple guards together with the rebuke, "Is this the way you answer the high priest?" But Jesus rises well above the blow and rebuke, and with commanding voice he responds, "If I have spoken wrongly, testify to the wrong; but if I have spoken rightly, why do you strike me?" And with that the interview finishes. Meanwhile Peter is in the courtyard denying his master.

In the morning Jesus is brought before Pilate, the Roman governor. Pilate intends to judge Jesus and, indeed, to do so with imperial style. Instead, Jesus judges Pilate. In the interchange between them, they virtually duel in sharp interchanges, but Jesus is clearly the stronger. Pilate wants to release him. Plainly, he is unsettled by Jesus, but to please the Jews he has Jesus scourged and then brought out before them. Yet then they call out for his crucifixion. The Jews explain that they want Jesus' death "because he made himself the Son of God." There are many levels of meaning, indeed confusion, around this statement as it emerges in the midst of the drama. Of course, it is true that Jesus is the Son of God. But the Jews understand it only as a blasphemy, and it frightens Pilate. We hear, "Now when Pilate heard this statement, he became even more afraid, and went back into the praetorium and said to Jesus, 'Where are you from?'" If asked in the proper way, this is the right question, the critical question. We have already heard the answer earlier in the gospel: Jesus has come from God and is returning to God. It is his hour. But Pilate does not ask the critical question with the right spirit, and Jesus refuses to answer. Pilate tries to act tough and pulls rank, saying, "Do you not speak to me? Do you not know that I have power to release you and I have power to crucify you?" What Pilate does not realize is that Jesus has infinitely higher rank. Jesus answers him, "You would have no power over me if it had not been given you from above," that is to say, from Jesus' Father or even from Jesus himself, for no one takes his life from him. He has "power to lay it down, and power to take it up again."

In the end Pilate hands Jesus over to be crucified, but he does so weakly and frustrated by the Jewish pressure that he is not strong enough to resist. Jesus, for his part, takes up the cross, and, the evangelist emphasizes, does so "by himself." He virtually marches out toward Golgotha. At this point in the story the narrator is swift and terse in what he tells us. Jesus' crucifixion is presented almost as an enthronement, for we are told that two others are crucified with him, Jesus in the middle. Above his head, Pilate has an inscription placed which proclaims in Latin, Greek, and Hebrew, "Jesus the Nazorean, the King of the Jews." The different languages indicate that the spectacle is there for all the world to see, and each person is faced with the challenge to understand it rightly. The Jews object that Pilate should have specified that Jesus only *claimed* to be King of the Jews. But Pilate answers, "What I have written, I have written."

Even in his last minutes Jesus is active in making providential arrangements for those he loves. He sees standing beside the cross his mother and the one described by the evangelist as "the disciple whom Jesus loved." This disciple is meant to represent us all. Seeing them, he says to his mother, "Woman, behold, your son," indicating to her the disciple. To the disciple he says, "Behold, your mother." On the literal level, we can hear these words as Jesus simply asking them to take care of one another, thoughtful last words from a devoted son. But their meaning is deeper, and Jesus is "fully aware" of how very much deeper. Jesus is asking his mother to take someone else as son in his place. We could rightly think that anyone else surely would be a poor substitute. But Jesus himself does not think so, because he alone understands how much of his own life he is pouring into his disciple's life as he dies. In his dying Jesus is giving us all that the Father has given to him. His dying can make of each disciple one whom his mother can truly recognize and love as her own child. And every disciple receives in the mother the very relationship that Jesus had with her. Generous, glorious dying!

To the very end Jesus shows himself to be quite conscious of all that he is doing and accomplishing. The evangelist says so explicitly. He says that Jesus is "aware that everything was now finished." He utters a brief sentence, not in desperation, but quite intentionally "in order that the Scripture might be fulfilled." He says, "I thirst." Of course, once again there is a literal level of meaning to the dying man's words. But the deeper level of meaning is that Jesus is thirsting for the faith of each one who follows the story and details of his death. We can use here the words of Jesus heard earlier in the gospel when he told the Samaritan woman at the well that he was thirsty and asked her for a drink. He said, "If you knew . . . who is saying to you, 'Give me a drink,' you would have asked him and he would have given you living water" (John 4:10). Jesus is dying to give us this living water, and he is thirsty for our belief from the cross. "Whoever believes in me, as scripture says, 'Rivers of living water will flow from within him'" (John 7:38).

Jesus' very last words show him still "aware" of everything. It is the Father's own Son who is truly at work on the cross, and now his work is done. He has fulfilled the "command I have received from my Father" (John 10:18), and so he declares, "It is finished." After these words the evangelist tells us that Jesus dies, but the language used to say this—still swift and terse—overflows with levels of meaning. We hear, "And bowing his head, he handed over the spirit." On the most literal level one can understand here that Jesus breathed his last breath. And that is what happened. Jesus stopped breathing. But what really happened when Jesus stopped breathing? What does faith discern? Faith discerns that the last breath of Jesus is his "handing over" the Spirit to the world, the pouring out of the Holy Spirit onto the world. His last breath is nothing less than the Spirit within him released now into all the world. His last breath is already Pentecost.

On Good Friday during the liturgy when the narrator sings or says the words, "And bowing his head, he handed over the spirit," the whole assembly falls on its knees and observes a profound silence. With this posture and in this awestruck silence the levels of meaning I am indicating here begin to emerge for us. We adore the God who shows himself to be holy, mighty, and immortal in this unimaginable way. We are on our knees and dare not utter a word as the Holy Spirit, released from Jesus' own body, begins to descend upon us, begins to move again in the world. The event of Jesus' dying converges with the event of this liturgy.

In a final remark in his account, John alone of all the evangelists shows us that even the dead body of Jesus is life-giving. We are told that a soldier thrust a lance into the side of the "already dead" Jesus. Then in reverential tones, we hear, "and immediately blood and water flowed out." The evangelist sees considerable significance in this detail and wants us to contemplate it. He immediately adds the comment, "An eyewitness has testified, and his testimony is true; he knows that he is speaking the truth, so that you also may come to believe." And he notes that a verse from Hebrew Scripture is fulfilled in this detail, a verse which mysteriously says, "They will look upon him whom they have pierced." What happens for us when we look upon the pierced body of Jesus and see blood and water immediately flowing out? We understand that the blood and water are indications of Eucharist and baptism, and we begin to see that these sacraments have their origin precisely here, in the death of Jesus. What for him is death is life for us. Indeed, the blood and water that began to flow when the soldier opened Christ's side have never stopped flowing. In that water we have each been baptized; of that blood we are continually given to drink in the Eucharist.

The General Intercessions

The general intercessions are the next part of the liturgy of Good Friday that we want to examine. Technically speaking, this is part of the Liturgy of the Word, the last part. That the Missal considers intercessions as part of the Liturgy of the Word means to indicate that this way of praying ought to be seen as emerging from the Scriptures we have heard. Today's Scriptures have been powerful, and the way of praying that emerges from them is equally powerful, equally big. In the intentions prayed for, we will recognize the kinds of concerns that are meant to shape the general intercessions that are part of any celebration of Mass. But the form of the prayer today is much more elaborate.

There are ten major intentions, and the prayer for each is divided into three parts. The first part is an invitation to pray, announced by the deacon or by a lay minister if there is no deacon. These invitations are carefully formulated. They instruct us in how to pray, what to pray for, and how to consider the persons and things we are praying for. After the invitation, the second part is silent prayer by all, either kneeling or standing. The space of our prayer here is inside the hour of Jesus' dying and his release of the Spirit into the world. We pray under the force of that Spirit. The third part of the prayer is the oration prayed by the priest. Whereas the deacon's words are addressed to the assembly, the priest's words are now directed to God the Father in the name of us all. The invitation and the silent prayer have been preparatory for this climax of the priest's prayer directly addressed to God. Ten times this pattern is repeated around ten different intentions. These prayers are called "General Intercessions" because the intentions are meant to sweep wide over virtually all the needs of the church and world. So we pray for the church, the Pope, and all the clergy. We pray for catechumens, for the unity of Christians, and for the Jewish people. We pray for those who do not believe in Christ and those who do not believe in God. And finally, we pray for those in public office and for all those with special needs.

Why do we have this elaborate form of prayer precisely on Good Friday? Why these prayers that try to cover so many needs and intentions? The answer lies in the theology we encountered in the reading from the Letter to the Hebrews. There we saw that Jesus' death on the cross is an entry into the heavenly sanctuary with his own blood where his sacrifice perpetually intercedes before God on our behalf.

These prayers give liturgical form to that perpetual intercession. Every prayer prayed by the priest begins with a direct address to God with the title "Almighty ever-living God," and every prayer ends "through Christ our Lord." This is the fundamental form of the prayer established by Jesus on the cross, "our great high priest." We are familiar, of course, with this form of prayer; it is always in this form that the church prays. But today's liturgy gives us a privileged vantage point from which to see how profound is the sense of what it means to address a prayer to God "through Christ our Lord." It is nothing less than putting the death of Jesus before the eyes of the Father as we enumerate our many needs and desires. In effect, we are saying to the Father that Jesus is asking this for us "with loud cries and tears" on our behalf. Could the Father refuse such a prayer, a prayer not merely made up of words but prayed with the whole thrust of Christ's body confidentially placed into the hands of the Father, "who was able to save him [and us!] from death"?

To move carefully through the ten prayers requires not a small amount of time. Standing and kneeling again ten different times can become tiresome, even irksome perhaps. Still, there is probably meant to be a lesson for us also in this dimension, the dimension of prayer that lasts too long. The death of Jesus also lasted too long. It was stretched out over six physically agonizing hours. The long prayer that we undertake at this point in the liturgy is an image precisely of that. Jesus wishes to associate us with himself in his work of intercession. From him, through the long hours of his dying, we learn that prayer is work. Prayer is suffering. Prayer is dying for others.

The Adoration of the Holy Cross

With the adoration of the cross we arrive at that part of the liturgy that is completely unique to this day. Nothing like it occurs in any other liturgy of the year. There are two basic parts to it. The first is a showing of the cross to all the people, and the second is a procession in which all come forward and one by one show some sign of veneration for the cross, usually a kiss.

Knowing something of the history of the development of this unique rite helps us to understand more precisely its meaning. It has its origins in the fourth-century church of Jerusalem. In that city the emperor Constantine's mother, St. Helen, had carried out extensive

investigations to discover the place of the actual death and burial of
Jesus and to recover, if possible, the actual cross on which he had been
crucified. She was believed to have succeeded in this, and thereafter
the Jerusalem liturgy, especially in its celebration of the Pasch, developed around a church built at the place of crucifixion and burial.
When we remember that the paschal liturgies, no matter where on
earth they are celebrated, are always a memorial of the concrete historical events of Jesus' death and resurrection, it is not difficult to
imagine how moving such liturgies would be in the very place where
those events originally took place. At the liturgy on Friday a large
piece of the wood of the cross was placed on the altar before the
people in such a way that they could come forward to venerate it.
This is the origin of the ritual that we still celebrate today. The way
we celebrate it today has its deepest roots in the Jerusalem liturgy,
and so describing its original shape can function also as a description
of the present form.

The Jerusalem liturgy had made its way to Rome by the end of the
seventh century. By this time fragments of the wood of the cross were
shared by the church of Jerusalem with other churches, and Rome
was certainly included among these. In fact the church of Santa Croce
(Holy Cross) in Rome was built as a shrine for the veneration of that
city's fragment. Rome was happy to adopt as its own the liturgy celebrated in Jerusalem on Good Friday. In the Middle Ages, small slivers
of this precious relic were shared among thousands of churches and
monasteries. Cynics have remarked that if all the fragments of the
so-called wood of the true cross were gathered together, it would
be enough wood to build at least a large house. But in fact someone
once investigated this a little more rigorously and concluded that
such fragments in fact would not be enough even to form a whole
cross. Whatever the actual authenticity of these fragments may be,
the meaning of the Jerusalem liturgy is clear enough. People believed
that on the very day on which Christ's death was remembered, they
were seeing, touching, and kissing the wood of the cross on which
he had hung. This would have been an extremely moving moment
of prayer and devotion. It would have been vivid, concrete contact
with a piece of the actual historical event of our salvation.

In the Roman liturgy, by the twelfth century, when the wood of
the true cross was brought before the people, it was at first covered
by a veil. Slowly and carefully a small portion of the veil was pulled

back, and, referring to what little of it could be seen, the bishop exclaimed in song, "Behold the wood of the cross on which hung the salvation of the world. Come, let us worship." Then all the people would fall on their knees in adoration. After this, the veil was pulled back a little further, exposing now a larger portion to view, and the same song was sung: "Behold the wood of the cross on which hung the salvation of the world. Come, let us adore." This continued until the wood was completely exposed. What is striking about the action and the words is that the emphasis and focus is on the actual wood. The dramatic unveiling of it, a little at a time, is nothing less than the slow unfolding of a divine revelation. It is an epiphany, a manifestation, a vision of God in the vision of the cross. What is seen is so holy and venerable that we must, as it were, accustom our vision to it in small doses.

After the cross was fully exposed to view, then the people would come forward to touch and venerate it. The sense of divine epiphany continues in the gestures, practices, words, and song that surround this veneration. Sometimes people would remove their shoes, in imitation of Moses before the epiphany of the burning bush, when he was told by God to remove his shoes because he was on "holy ground" (Exod 3:5). People would genuflect, sometimes more than once, as they progressively drew nearer to the holy cross. The words that were sung are a stunning example of cross and glory held in tension. An instrument of torture is held up to view, but the words of song express what faith discerns. They exclaim, "Holy is God! Holy and Mighty! Holy and Immortal One! Have mercy on us!" These are words with which one sings awareness of being in the presence of God, words of exclamation before a divine vision. The threefold repetition of the exclamation "Holy, Holy, Holy" has its original inspiration in Isaiah's vision of "the Lord seated on a high and lofty throne." In that vision described by the prophet, Seraphim with six wings were seen in the presence of the all-holy God. With two of these wings "they veiled their faces, with two they veiled their feet, and with two they hovered aloft. 'Holy, holy, holy is the LORD of hosts,' they cried to one another." (See Isa 6:1-4.) Now, for Christian faith, this vision of the holiness of God finds unexpected fulfillment in the vision of the wood of the cross.

The words "Holy is God! Holy and Mighty! Holy and Immortal One" were sung in Greek in the Jerusalem liturgy. In Rome, the Greek song was kept but also translated into Latin, and choruses would alternate the languages as the people continued their veneration. Even today, when vernacular versions of the same text are prepared, often the Latin and Greek continue to be sung as well. These are precious reminders for us of how ancient is the form of the liturgy we are celebrating.

Rightly every person present wanted to come forward to express devotion to the holy cross. So other chants were developed through the centuries to accompany what was inevitably a time-consuming procession. There is a set of chants called the Reproaches that alternated with the Greek and Latin "Holy is God!" chants. The Reproaches are called such because they are poetic texts in the prophetic style (see Micah 6:3) that give voice to what the dying of Jesus would "say" to us. They are haunting, sad melodies in which Jesus asks, "My people, my people, what have I done to you? How have I offended you? Answer me!" The verses are developed by recalling major scenes from Israel's salvation history, and then contrasting these with Jesus on the cross. For example, Jesus is heard to say, "I led you out of Egypt, from slavery to freedom, but you led your Savior to the cross." Or again, "I opened the sea before you, but you opened my side with a spear." Or, "For you I struck down the kings of Canaan, but you struck my head with a reed." We should note how swift and direct is the Christian exegesis of Old Testament images that occur in these formulations. The God who acts in Israel's past, referring to himself as "I," is the same "I" speaking in Jesus. Thus, the one on the cross is that same God. There are many such verses. These are heartbreaking meditations, for they help us to realize how absolutely horrifying are our sins which have led to Jesus' death, how deep our betrayal. They also place his death in the context of the whole history of Israel. God's mighty deeds on Israel's behalf, as Israel's own prophets again and again remind us, should have resulted in greater faithfulness and should never have resulted in the death of Jesus on the cross. Yet even so, Jesus loves to the end and—so the alternating chants show—precisely in the cross he is "Holy God! Holy Strong One! Holy Immortal One!"

Sometimes nowadays it is objected that the Reproaches are an anti-Semitic part of the liturgy and so should no longer be used. But this is to fail to realize how the Christian church understands herself in relation to Israel. Israel's history is our own. Her prophets' reproaches are addressed to us. Her guilt in the death of Jesus is our own. The mistake is to think that when the Scriptures or the liturgy say "Israel," it is only the Jewish people that is meant. But Christian faith understands that in the concrete history of Israel's dealings with God, there is found the pattern of us all in our dealings with God. I am the one addressed by Jesus on the cross. To me he says, "I exalted you with great power, and you hung me on the scaffold of the Cross." I am addressed by the cross, and everyone on earth is addressed. This is the faith of the church.

It is perhaps misleading to name these moving meditations "the Reproaches." That word is actually never used in the texts. And if we think about the conduct and attitude of Jesus during the hours of his death, it is striking that during all his mistreatment, he never utters a single reproach. It is not in fact Jesus who is reproaching as he dies. The words placed in his mouth in these texts are a poetic form by which in some sense we reproach ourselves by imagining what Jesus, so unjustly treated, could have said but, strikingly, did not.

As I mentioned, the shape of this liturgy as we have it today derives from the ancient forms developed in Jerusalem and Rome. Describing its past shape has served also to explain its present shape. There is, however, one option in the present Missal for the way the cross may be shown that we have not yet mentioned. Rather than progressively removing a veil and exposing the wood to view as was done in some of the ancient liturgies, it is possible to carry a cross, already uncovered, from the door of the church through the church and into the sanctuary, stopping at key points and singing, "Behold the wood of the cross on which hung the salvation of the world. Come, let us adore." Whichever of the two forms is used, the meaning is the same. What is shown, what is revealed, is precisely *wood*. And the showing is meant to be divine epiphany. In the vision we are meant to recognize God—holy, strong, and immortal. On a practical level then, it is not a crucifix—that is, a cross with the body of the Lord depicted on it—that is the object of veneration, but wood itself, ideally a sliver of the true cross placed somehow within a larger wood cross that holds the fragment. If this is not possible and a crucifix is used, it should always be made of wood.

I ask the reader to permit me to share a personal experience I had with the liturgy I have been describing here. At my monastery we have what is said to be a fragment of the true cross. On Good Friday we place this fragment within a large wooden reliquary shaped in the form of a cross. "This is the wood of the cross" that is exposed to view and for veneration. The sliver of the true wood touches the other wood and, as it were, renders all the wood to be that holy wood. Yet I must confess that through the years I had my doubts about the authenticity of our relic. I recognized the value of the ceremony in any case, but it was hard for me to believe that what I was kissing could truly be a small piece of the cross on which Jesus had actually died. I struggled with this doubt year by year as I made my way forward in the procession. Then one year the question suddenly struck me, "But what if it really is!?" I felt a kind of shock just considering the possibility. I thought, "My God, if it really is, what a precious relic then!" The instrument of my redemption, historical contact with my Lord, touching with my hand, my mouth, the wood on which he died! It seemed amazing to me. I kissed the wood that year—and have done the same in every subsequent year—full of love and gratitude, feeling in a new way how very concrete and substantial was the death of Jesus. I did not worry about authenticity after this. All wood, any wood, is on this day *that* wood—"the wood of the cross on which hung the salvation of the world." Celebrating that wood is the meaning of this remarkable part of the liturgy of Good Friday.

Holy Communion

The third and final part of the liturgy on this day is the reception of Holy Communion. We already spoke of the previous day's liturgy which finished with the procession of the Blessed Sacrament to the place of reposition. The Blessed Sacrament was reserved then so that it could be received on this day. This was necessary since, as we have already considered, the Eucharist is never celebrated on this day. The altar, which has remained unclothed throughout the liturgy to this point, is now covered with a cloth. The Blessed Sacrament is brought to the altar from the place of reposition by a deacon or priest. There is no elaborate procession. The mood is sober and quiet. All the people stand in silence. From a ritual point of view what follows is familiar enough. The Lord's Prayer is recited by all, together with the prayer attached to it at Mass, "Deliver us, Lord, from every evil . . ." The sign of peace is not given, and after a prayer said privately by the priest, he holds up the Blessed Sacrament for the people to see and announces, as at Mass, "Behold the Lamb of God . . ." The people say the usual prayer, "Lord, I am not worthy . . ." and then come forward for Communion.

I describe this as being familiar enough from a ritual point of view. It will be recognized as following the structure of the Communion rite during the Mass, minus the sign of peace. But if the structure of this part is familiar, perhaps the mood of the whole is not. It feels unusual to be praying the Lord's Prayer in this way and to be receiving Communion without the preceding parts of the Mass having been enacted first. The slight sense of liturgical disorientation that we feel is meant to be there. It is all part of the singular character and mood of this singular day.

In fact, during the centuries different practices regarding Communion on this day have been employed throughout the various liturgical families. As mentioned, the Eucharist itself was never celebrated and consequently, in some liturgical traditions, Communion was not received. In the Roman rite there were many centuries in which Communion was received and many others in which it was not. In the mid-1950s, the practice of receiving Communion on this day was taken up again after many centuries without it.

This current practice gives us an opportunity for a special insight into the mystery of the Eucharist. I have said before that in the liturgies of these days we do not pretend for a while that we do not know that Jesus is risen, thinking only of his death and burial on Friday and Saturday as a means of heightening the dramatic effect of the commemoration of his resurrection on Sunday. No, whenever Christians gather for prayer they gather because Jesus is risen. We have stressed that this too is the case on Good Friday as we remember the Lord's death. So every time I receive the Lord in the Blessed Sacrament, it is the risen Lord that I receive. There is no other. But receiving the Lord in the Blessed Sacrament on Good Friday, and doing so outside the normal context of the celebration of the Mass, can remind me in a very forceful way that the risen Lord whom I receive is risen in that very same body in which he was crucified. To receive the Body of Christ as my food is to receive the Body crucified—now risen. We are very near now to the liturgy of the previous evening, Holy Thursday, where the Lord gave us in the signs of the meal a means for interpreting the meaning of his death. Whenever I receive the Body of the Lord, I receive it in some sense from the cross. There is perhaps no day when this is so clear as on Good Friday. The words of St. Paul heard in yesterday's second reading have a new resonance for us today: "For as often as you eat this bread . . . you proclaim the death of the Lord" (1 Cor 11:26). His death is the inexhaustible source of life for us, and we proclaim precisely this by consuming his Body on the day of his death.

We saw in the previous section that precious indeed is the opportunity to express our devotion and gratitude to the Lord for his glorious dying by kissing the wood of the cross on which he died. Far more precious than the relic of the cross is that which touches our lips now. The very Body that was crucified and is now risen is given to us as food. By eating this food we share in his life-giving death and resurrection.

Chapter 7

The Paschal Vigil in the Holy Night

The title of this chapter is taken from the Roman Missal. For this liturgy, the Missal begins with a comparatively ample set of rubrics, which should not surprise us since the Mass for this night is the biggest and most complex set of rituals that the church celebrates at any point in the liturgical year. Rubrics may not seem of immediate interest to the average reader, but often, and certainly here, the instructions they contain embody very condensed pieces of theology. It will be worth our looking at some of them briefly.

The rubrics begin by claiming that the Vigil about to be described and celebrated reflects "most ancient tradition." They call it the "greatest and most noble of all solemnities." They describe four parts, an outline that we'll follow below. The *first part* is called the Lucernarium and Easter Proclamation. These are tightly connected in meaning to the *second part* where "Holy Church meditates on the wonders the Lord God has done for his people from the beginning, trusting in his word and promise." More briefly it could have simply said "the Liturgy of the Word," but this longer description succinctly makes clear the purpose of this extended Liturgy of the Word. It is meditation. The key is the "wonders" of the Lord which have always accompanied his people and which contain a promise to trust in. Indeed, that promise will be fulfilled in the liturgy of this night. This long Liturgy of the Word is meant to infuse the passing of time of this night with a sense of waiting "until, as day approaches, with new members reborn in Baptism (the *third part*), the church is called to the table the Lord has prepared for his people, the memorial of his Death and Resurrection until he comes again (the *fourth part*)." We note that the climax is Eucharist, that is, "the memorial of his Death and Resurrection"—Pasch as Passion and Pasch as Passage in one single liturgy.

One of the rubrics also states that the entire Vigil "must take place during the night, so that it begins after nightfall and ends before daybreak on the Sunday." Why this clear and insistent directive? It helps to ensure that we taste the mystery of this special night. Jesus' rising from the dead did not take place at dawn on Easter Sunday; dawn revealed that something had happened in deepest night. The resurrection is a deed worked by God in darkness, with no human witnesses to the moment or the how of its happening. Throughout this long liturgy there will be a play between the night that surrounds us and a new kind of light that begins to shine from within its darkest depths. It is the new light of resurrection. With darkness established as the context of our celebration, we can turn now to the first part, which in the Missal carries two titles.

First Part:
The Solemn Beginning of the Vigil or Lucernarium

Fire

Here too a striking rubric meets us. We read, "A blazing fire is prepared in a suitable place outside the church." That is, not just any fire or tame little flame. What is envisioned is something impressive and conspicuous, in Latin a *rogus ardens*. The fire is to stand out—beautiful, dangerous, and impressive—against darkest night. The prayers and actions that follow show that this fire is nothing less than an encounter with the risen Lord and the light that shines from his resurrection. It is he that is beautiful, dangerous, and impressive.

The priest begins with a brief instruction which in fact is an excellent summary of the meaning of the whole elaborate liturgy that is to follow. He refers to the moment as "this most sacred night in which our Lord Jesus Christ passed over from death to life." It is into that event that this liturgy splices us. It does so by means of what is called "the memorial of the Lord's paschal solemnity." Here, once again, it is important to catch all the dimensions of the terms *paschal* and *memorial*. Liturgy remembers, and by remembering comes under the force of the deed of God that is remembered. Here the supreme deed of God, the Pasch, is the object of the memorial. The instruction explains that this liturgical memorial has two dimensions: "listening to his word and celebrating his mysteries." This refers to the long Liturgy of the Word (part 2) and to the celebration of the sacraments or mysteries of baptism (part 3) and Eucharist (part 4). By making this memorial, ". . . we shall have the sure hope of sharing his triumph over death and living with him in God." After the instruction the priest blesses the fire.

The Paschal Candle

Then the paschal candle is brought to him for its preparation. The rubrics designate a specific set of symbols to decorate the large candle, and these begin to define the candle's meaning. Shortly after, the singing of the *Exsultet* will do this the more. The candle, which will be lit from the blazing fire, is clearly a symbol of the risen Christ but not in a vague sense. It will symbolize the resurrection of one who has been crucified, of a sacrificial death that gives light to a darkened world. So a cross is traced on the candle, while the priest slowly says the words, "Christ yesterday and today, the Beginning and the End." He writes the first and last letters of the Greek alphabet on the top and the bottom of the cross, saying, "the Alpha and the Omega." These are divine and timeless titles of Christ, and they appear, they are revealed, precisely by his cross. The titles are taken from the Letter to the Hebrews (13:8) and the book of Revelation (1:8; 21:6; 22:13). In Revelation these phrases are found on the lips of the risen Lord who appears in glorious epiphanies. The decoration of the cross continues by slowly marking the four numerals of the current year into the four corners of the cross while the priest slowly says the words, "All time belongs to him and all the ages. To him be glory and power through every age and for ever. Amen." With these words and signs the church entrusts her passing moment in history, designated by the year, to the timeless and ever-present sacrifice of Christ. The death and resurrection of Christ is *the* central event of all time and history, and it draws all other events to itself, absorbs all other events into itself.

Then five grains of incense are inserted into the cross on the candle. These grains are often designed as nails, and the five places in which they are inserted remember the five wounds of Christ's feet, hands, and side. As they are placed, the priest slowly says, "By his holy and glorious wounds, may Christ the Lord guard us and protect us." The Risen One, whose light will flame from this candle, is precisely the one who was crucified. Strikingly, the wounds are called "holy and glorious." The prayer that the wounds would "guard and protect us" is an allusion to the paschal lamb, whose blood protected the houses of the Israelites from the destroying angel on the night of the exodus. This night is that same night.

Procession

The candle is then lit from the blazing fire, and incense is prepared as well from the fire. At the door of the church, the candle is held high by a deacon and smoke goes up around it. Though no explicit explanation is offered, we are meant to think of the pillar of fire and the cloud by which Israel was led out of Egypt. Now Christ is that pillar and cloud, and it is we who are led out of the Egypt of sin and death into life in his church. This is, here and now, his Pasch. The deacon lets the light, the cloud, and the experience of the procession speak for themselves. He declares only the simple words, "The Light of Christ." Then the light is spread from the one candle to many candles held in the hands of every member of the assembly. As the assembly fills the darkened space, the church fills with light. This is, here and now, Christ's Pasch. Clearly we share in it. His light invades us, and the darkness which had surrounded us is victoriously shut out and conquered.

The Easter Proclamation (Exsultet)

Next the magnificent, long poem, known as the *Exsultet* (from its first word in the original Latin), is sung. The *Exsultet* is an extraordinary balance of Pasch as *passion* and Pasch as *passage*. Taking account of the intense atmosphere created by all that has taken place so far and the church filled with light from this paschal candle, I will comment here on the structure of the *Exsultet* and many of its phrases. This text and its context give us a privileged opportunity to develop further our understanding of the resurrection.

From the words and actions that have happened around the fire and candle, and now in the content of the *Exsultet*, it is evident already that this Vigil is not simply a celebration and announcement of the resurrection. As a liturgy it is a profoundly detailed and nuanced interweaving of the themes of life-giving and glorious *passion* and life-giving and glorious *resurrection*.

After the deacon incenses the candle—making the pillar of fire and the cloud to appear clearly in the center of this assembly—he sings insistently, "Exult, exult, rejoice, rejoice." The hosts of heaven and angelic ministers are invited to exult. Earth too is urged to be glad, all the corners of the earth. And the church too is urged to rejoice. So heaven, earth, and church are joined together, "arrayed with the lightning of his glory." Even the very structure within which we stand in this new light receives an urgent command: "let this holy building shake with joy." Plainly the point is that the entire cosmos is involved in the event that is underway. Yes, and something immensely joyful is happening right here and now and within the very building in which we stand.

After this introduction, we briefly exchange a familiar dialogue, the same one that opens the preface of the eucharistic prayer: "The Lord be with you." "Lift up your hearts." "Let us give thanks to the Lord our God." By its threefold responses, the assembly is taken into the prayer, which is sung as thanksgiving in their name, for they have answered that "it is right and just" to do so.

Next follows the main body of this intensely theological and effusive poem in song. The dialogue has already established that it is a poem of thanksgiving. The object of thanksgiving will be God's huge deed of the Pasch, understood both as passion and passage. The text urges that the song be sung and listened to with "ardent love of mind and heart and with devoted service of our voice." This is a reminder that our access to the reality of resurrection can be had only with these qualities, with our own sincere involvement in the celebration. We wish "to acclaim our God invisible, the almighty Father, and Jesus Christ, our Lord, his Son, his Only Begotten." Referring to the Father's invisible nature implies without saying so that through his Son, through the Son's visible deeds, the Father is contacted and known. The titles of the Son are piled up: "Jesus Christ, our Lord, his Son, his Only Begotten." We feel the intensity of the relationship of Father and Son, the Son's closeness to the Father—"*his* Son, *his* Only Begotten"—and his closeness to us—"*our* Lord."

Next follows what is typical of Jewish and Christian prayer—namely, a memorial, a liturgical recounting of the deeds of the past that are being celebrated here and now. Everything is concentrated now on Jesus Christ and how the Father is working through him. The action of Christ is first described as taking place in the context of its consequences for the whole of humanity, for he is portrayed as the one "who for our sake paid Adam's debt to the eternal Father and, pouring out his own dear Blood, wiped clean the record of our ancient sinfulness." The image of pouring out blood clearly is an image of Pasch as passion. What is celebrated is Christ's sacrifice, and the poet allows an expression of how precious it is by calling it "his own dear blood." We should note how the present assembly celebrating is included in this vision of humanity's redemption by the use of the word "our": it is for "our sake," and it is the record of "our ancient sinfulness" that is wiped away.

The next strophe begins with the joyful pronouncement that "These, then, are the feasts of Passover." The English word "Passover" translates the Latin *paschalia*. And the first image of the feast that is given comes to us from Exodus 12, where, as we have seen, the celebrations and images of both Holy Thursday and Good Friday are very much rooted. So those celebrations of the Triduum are still present to us in this, the Triduum's climax. The text calls these the paschal feasts "in which is slain the Lamb, the one true Lamb, whose Blood anoints the doorposts of believers." Israel's exodus is directly recalled with these images, but it is seen as fulfilled in Christ, "the one true Lamb," and it is Christ's being slain and his blood that is celebrated now.

The images of the next several strophes are taken from Exodus 14, where Pasch is presented as passage. We hear a phrase that will repeat itself some five times—"This is the night,"—each time recalling, in liturgical memorial, deeds of God in Israel's past. But the present tense of the phrase helps us realize that God's deeds from the past are present to us still in this very liturgy, and in fact those past deeds of Israel's exodus all converge in the night of Christ's being raised from the dead and the night of this Vigil liturgy being celebrated. So this assembly sings of "our forebears, Israel's children" and recalls this as the night of their passage through the Red Sea. It recalls it as the night "that with a pillar of fire banished the darkness of sin." And with insistence it calls this the night that is being celebrated by Christians "throughout the world" with the result that the exodus passage ultimately finds its fulfillment in the moral passage that separates Christians "from worldly vices and the gloom of sin, leading them to grace and joining them to his holy ones." This is a reference, among other things, to the celebration of baptism and Eucharist that will take place within the same liturgy of this holy night. And all this climaxes with a direct reference to the resurrection, the deed of God in this holy night. It declares, "This is the night when Christ broke the prison-bars of death and rose victorious from the underworld." All the events of the exodus converge and are drawn into this climax: from the lamb slain in this night, to passing through the sea dry-shod in this night, to the pillar of fire that banishes the darkness of sin in this night, to the night in which Christ rose victorious from the grave. "This is the night" in which this very liturgy is being celebrated, and all the force and power of resurrection is made present and actual for the gathered assembly.

After arriving at this direct proclamation of resurrection as climax within the poem, the poem shifts its style from the liturgical memorial of the deeds of God to what we could call a contemplative assessment and meditation on what all this means for us. It is theology in poetry, and it provides us with yet more occasion to develop here an understanding of the resurrection from within the liturgical experience. A number of paradoxical statements or unexpected contrasts form the structure of the poetic expression.

The first of these declares, "Our birth would have been no gain, had we not been redeemed." This is a bold declaration that our life would be futile were it not for all that is achieved for us by the death and resurrection of Christ. The exaggeration is intentional, saying that it would be better never to have been born unless we can enjoy the new life we are celebrating in this night. The Father is directly addressed by the exclamation "O wonder of your humble care for us!" And we declare to him that we grasp the immensity of his love. "O love, O charity beyond all telling, to ransom a slave you gave away your Son." The contrast between slave and Son puts into clear relief how astounding is what has been done for us. The Father has given away for our sake what is most precious to him—his Son—and the Son has willingly let himself be given away for us. This is quite concretely the shape of "love beyond all telling."

The next phrases are even more theologically daring. The poet exclaims, "O truly necessary sin of Adam, destroyed completely by the death of Christ!" This says something to the effect of "Thank God Adam sinned because it provoked such an enormously generous response from God." Mention of the death of Christ places before us yet again the understanding of Pasch as passion, and the theological declaration is made that this "destroyed completely" the sin of Adam. This daring line of theology is insisted upon in the next phrase: "O happy fault that earned so great, so glorious a Redeemer!" The "logic" of these stunning paradoxes is rooted, first, in the need for us to understand the fact that the sin of Adam and his fault could be nothing other than something that we should deeply regret. It is impossible to think that it is something we could be glad about. All this is true. But God's love and mercy is infinitely bigger than this valid and correct assessment of sin. It is shown us in "so great, so glorious a Redeemer."

The next set of paradoxical statements or unexpected contrasts is developed by returning to the theme of "this night." We see again how vital it is that this liturgy is celebrated in the night. The night itself is one of the fundamental symbols of this whole liturgy and so a symbol that will enable us to understand and penetrate a mysterious dimension of the way in which we experience the reality of the resurrection. The word "night" is repeated again and again to drive home the paradox. "O truly blessed night," the poet exclaims, and again declares the resurrection in striking images. The night is "worthy alone to know the time and hour when Christ rose from the underworld." I mentioned above that it takes place in the night because the resurrection itself occurred in the night and that the dawn of Easter morning simply reveals that something had already happened in the night. Part of the resurrection mystery is that in itself it cannot be seen, just as nothing can be seen in the night. But that it cannot be seen does not mean that nothing happens. Resurrection happens at a time and in a way known only to God. But that it does indeed happen is what renders this night "truly blessed."

Next, the phrase "this is the night" is taken up again, suggesting that a text from Old Testament Scripture (Ps 139:11-12) is fulfilled beyond all imagining in the meaning of this night: "This is the night of which it is written: the night shall be as bright as day, dazzling is the night for me and full of gladness." We can feel more forcefully the power of these claims if we remind ourselves of two things about the ancient culture in which this poem was originally produced. First, that culture experienced a scriptural text that was fulfilled in a surprising way as a moment of great epiphany. The insight was received with delight, with a person saying something to the effect of, "Who could have imagined that the ultimate meaning of the text would be this?" The second thing to which the ancient culture would have been more sensitive is the sense that night is, because of its darkness, quite dangerous. So the contrast drawn here is unexpectedly strong. Instead of being dark and laden with fear, the resurrection makes this night "bright as day, dazzling, full of gladness."

Then there follows a striking claim about "the sanctifying power of this night." The sense of a moral passage is the content of the claim, and no less than seven marvelous results are produced in us by this "sanctifying power." They can surely be understood in reference to what will be effected in the coming celebration of baptism, but they are present already now as we stand in the light of this night and listen to what is declared. The power of this night "dispels wickedness, washes faults away, restores innocence to the fallen, and joy to mourners, drives out hatred, fosters concord, and brings down the mighty." When we encounter, in the Scriptures or in the liturgy, a list like this of one thing after another, we have to be sure we hear all that is said rather than just come away with a vague sense of it all being more or less the same thing. The litany of absolutely amazing things is meant to leave us startled by the inexhaustible nature of all that can be said and experienced in the reality we are caught up in.

Following this, the song turns our attention to the candle itself and its flame, addressing the Father and calling the night "your night of grace, O holy Father." The prayer asks the Father to "accept this candle, a solemn offering, the work of bees and of your servants' hands. . . ." This mention of bees may strike us as an odd and distracting detail. What can it possibly mean? Again, ancient listeners would have been quicker than we to catch the significance and to delight in it. It is a reference to the very material out of which the candle is made. Beeswax—something quite strange and useful—is discovered in the creation and through human ingenuity—"the work of your servants' hands"—becomes a candle that burns with the light of Christ's resurrection. The theological conclusion we are meant to draw is that with the right human touch the whole of the created order is made to declare the story of Christ's death and resurrection. We do and say something similar in the eucharistic liturgy with the bread and wine, drawing attention to the very material out of which they are made and the human ingenuity that makes them food and drink, calling them "fruit of the earth . . . fruit of the vine and work of human hands."

We pray that God will accept the candle as "a solemn offering, an evening sacrifice of praise." How can a candle be an offering, a sacrifice? It can because it represents Christ. Here we must recall the words and symbols with which the candle was prepared at the beginning of Mass. Christ's cross and wounds were etched into the wax that now burns. It gives light by being consumed. This is the sacrifice and offering. It is offered to the Father. The Son is consumed to ransom a slave. It is offered in "this night" and so becomes "the evening sacrifice" that fulfills all the evening sacrifices that filled Israel's religion. Now it is offered and called "this gift from your most holy Church." We can dare refer to ourselves before the Father as "your most holy Church" because Christ lets the church join with him in the offering of his sacrifice to the Father, just as we offer this burning candle in its act of being consumed.

Now the song turns to the fact that each member of the assembly gathered around this flaming pillar has a candle that was lit from it. The text celebrates that what the candle represents is shared among us all. It is called "fire into many flames divided, and yet never dimmed by sharing of its light." Yet another paradox is expressed here. Normally to divide is to lessen, to share is to have less. Not so with resurrection light. It brightens by sharing, by being consumed. And the beeswax again proclaims this cosmic paradox. The poem celebrates that the light is undimmed because in every hand the flame "is fed by melting wax, drawn out by mother bees to build a torch so precious." Pasch as suffering passion and Pasch as glorious passage are displayed now in perfect balance in this marvelous vision of an assembly surrounded by darkest night outside and yet standing inside within the radiance of the light of resurrection.

This night is a wedding of heaven and earth, just as a bride and groom in the dark of night consummate the bright explosion of their love. Christ's death and resurrection is the "wedding feast of the Lamb," and this is the Lamb's wedding night. "O truly blessed night, when things of heaven are wed to those of earth, and divine to the human."

Such intensity can hardly continue, and so the poem moves quickly toward its close with a request made to God. The word "therefore" links the preceding with the request that follows. "Therefore, O Lord, we pray that this candle," which burns so beautifully and with so much force, "may persevere undimmed, to overcome the darkness of this night." With this line we look from the night toward the dawn of the coming day and pray that the light from the candle within whose radiance we stand will "mingle with the lights of heaven." The light of heaven is light from Christ, likened to the sun itself as "the one Morning Star who never sets." We know the fragile flame we hold in our hands will burn out unless it mingles with this true light that never fades. That is the light into which we step on Easter morning. It is Christ himself, "who, coming back from death's domain, has shed his peaceful light on humanity, and lives and reigns for ever and ever."

Second Part: The Liturgy of the Word

The second part of the Vigil liturgy is an extended Liturgy of the Word in which nine readings are provided, seven from the Old Testament, a reading from the Letter to the Romans, and one of the Synoptic gospel accounts of resurrection. This obviously takes a considerable amount of time. As the rubrics tell us, the character of the Vigil "demands an extended period of time." This period creates a mood shift from the intensity, joy, and mysterious light of the *Exsultet*. The priest's exhortation at the beginning of this part indicates the mood and purpose of what is to follow. He urges the congregation, "now that we have begun our solemn Vigil, let us listen with quiet hearts to the Word of God." What has preceded has been strong, exuberant, full of vivid processions, song, incense, and candle flame. Now a quiet heart is called for. The priest continues by calling us to deep reflection, saying, "Let us meditate how in times past God saved his people and in these, the last days, has sent us his Son as our Redeemer." These words provide the clue for how we are to listen to and ponder the Scriptures we will hear. We hear God's saving deeds for Israel in the past as reaching their climax in what is called "these last days," when God acts definitively in his Son (see Joel 2:28 as in Acts 2:17 and Heb 1:2).

Seven Old Testament Readings

The seven long readings from the Old Testament, followed by a passage on baptism from the Letter to the Romans, create in detail a context for hearing what is the climax of this Liturgy of the Word, the solemn proclamation of the gospel of the resurrection. Resurrection is the point toward which all of God's past deeds point. Everything is driving toward that, and that is how we are meant to hear them, how we are meant to "meditate" on them. But the church makes her way not only to the resurrection gospel by way of these readings but also to baptism, which is the part of the Vigil liturgy to follow.

Each of the seven passages from the Old Testament is meant to represent a key epoch in the long history of God's dealings with Israel. These passages effect in the listening assembly an experience of itself moving through all these epochs. There is a wealth of material here. The scope of this book does not permit entering into it in detail. Nonetheless, it should be noted that these passages are among the key texts of the Old Testament that the Christian community has always used to understand Christ's death and resurrection as the fulfillment of all the deeds and promises of God. Each reading in its own way can be interpreted as patterning in advance the mystery of Pasch as passion and Pasch as passage.

Let's consider briefly the significance of each, both in terms of the resurrection (to be proclaimed in the gospel reading) and in terms of baptism (which will follow). Each reading is followed by a responsorial psalm, which deepens the sense of the reading and lets the community sing its joy and involvement in the passages it has just heard. Then each psalm is followed by a prayer led by the priest. Each of these prayers focuses in a very explicit way on the christological and liturgical sense of the scriptural text and clearly expresses the reason for its presence in this liturgy. The christological sense is the Lord's death and resurrection. The liturgical sense is baptism and Eucharist that will follow. Baptism and Eucharist are our primary means of communion in Christ's death and resurrection.

The first reading is the long creation account that opens the entire Bible in the book of Genesis. The creation itself is about *passage*, a passage from formless chaos to an ordered world, a passage where wind—or Spirit!—moves over shapeless, dangerous waters and brings forth light, life, and beauty. This is a prophecy of the pattern of the new creation that occurs in Christ's own passage from death to life. Christ's passage affects the whole of creation, as the responsorial psalm suggests in its refrain: "Lord, send out your Spirit, and renew the face of the earth." The prayer that follows contrasts "the world's creation in the beginning" with "the end of the ages," calling the former "marvelous" but the latter even more marvelous, for it is characterized as the time when "Christ our Passover has been sacrificed." This last phrase is a direct quotation of 1 Corinthians 5:17, which in Latin clearly expresses the connection with Pasch: *Pascha nostrum immolatus est Christus*. This is Pasch as *passion*. This night's Vigil is the new creation in Christ, and it is "the end of the ages" opening already now. The whole creation culminates in Christ our Passover sacrificed.

The second reading tells the story of how Abraham prepared to sacrifice his son Isaac. The mention of Abraham evokes the whole Abraham cycle of stories and the promise to him that he would be the father of many nations. In this promise Israel's whole existence is founded. This story shows us Pasch as *passion*. The relationship between Abraham and his son Isaac, as he prepares to immolate him in obedience to God's command, is a mysterious foreshadowing of the sacrifice of God the Father who "so loved the world that he gave his only Son" (John 3:16). Both Isaac and Jesus are innocent victims. Both ascend a mountain for sacrifice. Both carry the wood on which they will be offered. And in the end both are spared by the action of God. The responsorial psalm lets us understand its words as Isaac's prayer: "[Y]ou will not abandon my soul to the netherworld" (Ps 16:10). But these words are ultimately fulfilled in Christ's resurrection, as Peter's homily on Pentecost directly claims (Acts 2:25-33). The prayer that follows addresses God as "[you] who through the Paschal Mystery make Abraham the Father of many nations." This refers to the baptism(s) which will take place in this very night, as the present tense of the verb *make* (*efficis*) renders clear. In all the baptized throughout all the world in every age, the promise made to Abraham is fulfilled through the paschal sacrament.

The third reading is from Exodus 14, the key scriptural text that we have already discussed. This reading is so essential an element of the proclamation of Scripture in this holy night that, whereas the rubrics reluctantly allow eliminating some of the readings for "pastoral reasons," they require that, "Never, moreover, should the reading of chapter 14 of Exodus with its canticle be omitted." Why? The reason lies in how both Exodus 12 and Exodus 14 form and shape the fundamental consciousness of Israel as a nation saved by God from slavery in Egypt. These two passages form the content of the Passover feast, and it is in the context of the events of this feast that Jesus himself enters and undergoes his own Pasch. So just as the whole Triduum opens on Holy Thursday with the proclamation of Exodus 12, so now in the Vigil Exodus 14 is given a privileged place inside the long Liturgy of the Word. Now all its images are heard as a revelation of what is happening here and now in the event of this liturgy. The *Exsultet* has already proclaimed some of these images. This is the night when *we* "pass dry-shod through the Red Sea." This is the night "that with a pillar of fire banished the darkness of sin."

The text is meant especially to be heard as an image and foreshadowing of the baptism that will follow. The prayer after the responsorial makes this very clear. In fact two prayers are offered in the Missal as an option. The first of these addresses God as one whose ancient wonders remain undimmed even in our own day and then, remembering how God freed a single people from "Pharaoh's persecution," it declares him to be now "bringing about the salvation of the nations through the waters of rebirth." It prays that "the whole world may become children of Abraham and inherit Israel's birthright." The second prayer declares that "the Red Sea prefigures the sacred font and the nation delivered from slavery foreshadows the Christian people." The pattern of reading-responsorial-prayer that recurs seven times in this part of the Vigil shimmers with particular force in this instance. We are at the heart of the memorial of God's deeds of old converging with the here and now of this gathered assembly. The sung responsorial puts on the assembly's lips the very song that the Israelites sang on the other side of the Sea at which they arrived with Pharaoh's forces drowned behind them. Now those same words can be sung by all the baptized who follow Christ in his definitive passage from death to new life.

The fourth reading is from the book of Isaiah, an intense poetic oracle that speaks of Israel's misfortunes being reversed by God's unimaginable closeness and clemency. Images of marriage are used to express this. With awe the prophet expresses that "[t]he One who has become your husband is your Maker." The context is of a sinful situation reversed. "The LORD calls you back / like a wife forsaken . . . but with great tenderness I will take you back." This language and its images intensify, and all are used now as images for the resurrection in this night which reverses sinful humanity's situation. Of this reversal the Lord's voice says, "In an outburst of wrath, for a moment / I hid my face from you; / but with enduring love I take pity on you." This love is called "a covenant of peace" that will never be shaken. And if all this is language for resurrection, it means that it is also language for baptism, our share in resurrection. Every Christian shares in this covenant of peace. Every Christian is joined as if in marriage to the Maker and Creator of the universe, "the LORD of hosts . . . called God of all the earth." We recall the words of the *Exsultet*: "O truly blessed night, when things of heaven are wed to those of earth, and divine to the human." The responsorial celebrates with wonderment this reversal of the sinful predicament. "I will praise you, Lord, for you have rescued me." The movement is from death to resurrection: "O LORD, you brought me up from the netherworld; / you preserved me from among those going down into the pit." Christ himself sings these words in this holy night, and every baptized Christian joins him in this song.

The fifth reading is also from Isaiah, and begins with the Lord's own voice saying in invitation, "All you who are thirsty, / come to the water!" In the context of this liturgy we cannot help but hear this as an invitation to the waters of baptism. This is nothing less than a direct invitation for us to share in the risen life of the Lord emerging from the darkness of this night. The invitation continues: "[C]ome, receive grain and eat; / come, without paying and without cost, / drink wine and milk!" This is invitation to Eucharist, in which the sacrament of baptism finds its culmination, in which resurrection is shared with us in a magnanimous banquet. The Lord's generous words continue to pile up one after another. This is an hour of encounter with him that is called "a covenant renewed," and we hear the image of many nations running to Israel. The conversion of one's manner of life that baptism requires is also proclaimed: "Seek the LORD while he may be found, / call him while he is near. / Let the scoundrel forsake his way . . . [and] turn to the LORD for mercy." We sense as we listen that we are caught up this night in a deed of God unimaginable in its scope and surprise. "As high as the heavens are above the earth, / so high are my ways above your ways / and my thoughts above your thoughts," says the Lord. It is happening here and now to us, as the responsorial sings, addressing this assembly as the city of Zion: "Shout with exultation, O city of Zion, / for great in your midst / is the Holy One of Israel!"

The sixth reading is from the book of Baruch and develops further the theme of conversion that coming to baptism requires. The assembly is addressed as "Israel" and is rebuked for having "forsaken the fountain of wisdom." Wisdom was precisely God's gift to Israel: "[God] has traced out the whole way of understanding, / and has given her to Jacob, his servant, / to Israel, his beloved son." Now we are urged to take it up again, and baptism and its renewal will be the precise way in which we do so. This is how we are to hear the prophet's invitation, an invitation to an authentic Christian life: "Turn, O Jacob, and receive her: / walk by her light toward splendor. . . . Blessed are we, O Israel; / for what pleases God is known to us!" This last phrase is something splendid. We should not take it for granted. The prophet proclaims with wonder that God has revealed to us how we can conduct ourselves in such a way as to please him. The responsorial expresses in joyful song what all this means for us: "Lord, you have the words of everlasting life." These are the words that Peter addressed in loving adherence to Jesus when other disciples were breaking from Jesus on account of his challenging teaching about Eucharist. Peter said, "Master, to whom shall we go? You have the words of eternal life" (John 6:68). We echo Peter's words to express our own adherence to Jesus' challenge.

The seventh and final Old Testament reading is from the book of Ezekiel. The prophet delivers an oracle of the Lord in strong language that is meant to be heard, in the context of this night, as referring to baptism and to all the ways in which our participation in this liturgy effects for us a share in Christ's resurrection. So, again it is our particular assembly that is addressed when the Lord declares, "I will take you away from among the nations . . . and bring you back to your own land. I will sprinkle clean water upon you to cleanse you from all your impurities, . . . I will give you a new heart and place a new spirit within you, . . . you shall be my people, and I will be your God." In its original historical context, the prophet's oracle referred to the return of Israel from its exile in Babylon, an act of mercy on the part of God that was seen as restoring the covenant relation that Israel's sins had profaned. Now the oracle is understood as being fulfilled in a way that far exceeds the literal return from Babylon to Jerusalem. As the prayer after the responsorial states: "the pages of both Testaments instruct and prepare us to celebrate the Paschal Mystery." We pray that we may comprehend God's mercy "so that the gifts we receive from you [from God] this night may confirm our hope of the gifts to come."

The Gloria

Next the assembly will experience a noticeable shift in the energy of the liturgy. The rubrics direct that the altar candles be lit, the Gloria intoned, and all the bells of the church be rung while this hymn is sung. There is something exhilarating in all this: light, the joyful noise of bells, and exuberant song all emerging together from the dark night. We do well to note that the first words of this hymn are the words of the angelic choirs that sounded on another joyful night, the night when Christ was born and angels appeared to shepherds to announce the Good News of his birth. Now in this night what Christ was born to accomplish is revealed as having come to pass, and the song we sing is chanted together with angels who fill our assembly and strengthen our song. In the middle of the hymn Christ is directly addressed with a spilling over of one title after another. He is called "Lord Jesus Christ, Only Begotten Son, Lord God, Lamb of God, Son of the Father." We are familiar with this hymn, but in this night we should freshen our sense of its force and realize that these many titles are ultimately given to Jesus because of all that is accomplished in his death and resurrection. The language first emphasizes Pasch as passion. He is the "Lamb of God who takes away the sins of the world," a phrase repeated twice, and he is "seated at the right hand of the Father." The Lamb that was slain is glorified, and he is hymned as the One who alone is Holy, the One who alone is Lord, the One who alone is the Most High, with the Holy Spirit, in the glory of God the Father. Pasch as passion and Pasch as passage to the Father's right hand—sung by angels in the highest and on earth a gift of peace to people of good will.

From the Letter to the Romans

After a collect a passage from the Letter of Paul to the Romans (Rom 6:3-11) is read. This passage describes baptism as the means by which we have a share in the death and resurrection of Christ. In fact Paul's words here have had considerable impact on the way in which the Christian community developed its understanding of the theology of baptism and of sacraments in general, and so it merits our careful attention within the scope of this book's whole aim of examining resurrection in Scripture, liturgy, and theology.

First, a rhetorical question is posed by Paul to the Roman community: "Are you unaware that we who were baptized into Christ Jesus were baptized into his death?" Obviously this question, delivered originally to first-century Romans, is immediately and directly relevant to us as well, especially as we hear it inside a Vigil liturgy that will soon involve the celebration of baptism and the renewal of baptismal vows. A rhetorical question is meant to have an obvious answer. In this case, it would be something to the effect of, "Of course we aware of this!" Even so, when I hear this question, I often feel required to confess for myself and others that we are not really as aware as we ought to be of the enormous importance of what is being said here.

The word "baptism" in its most original sense means "to plunge." So the claim is that we have been plunged into the death of Christ. Paul's next sentence develops this, adding the idea of also being buried with Christ. All this is enacted through the ritual act of plunging. "We were indeed buried with him through baptism into death." And this ritual causes to happen in our own lives what happened in Christ's death and resurrection. Our being plunged—baptized—is "so that, just as Christ was raised from the dead by the glory of the Father, we too might live in newness of life."

Christ's own death, burial, and resurrection are in no way a ritual act. They are the huge deed of God that effects our salvation. Baptism, by contrast, is a ritual act; but it is for us a means of communion in the divine deed. Paul explains how this works. He begins by saying, "[I]f we have grown into union with him through a [likeness of his death] . . ." He calls baptism "a likeness of his death." (I am translating closely from the Greek.) This word *likeness* (in Greek, *homoion*) becomes a technical word in Christian vocabulary for the sacraments. Ritually a sacrament is a *likeness* to something else—the larger reality—to which it refers. The larger reality is the actual death and resurrection of Christ. Baptism is a likeness of this because it involves a plunging, which corresponds to Christ's dying and being buried. One also comes up from the plunge, which corresponds to Christ's rising. And so Paul's whole sentence reads, "[I]f we have grown into union with him through a [likeness of his death], we shall also be united with him in the resurrection."

Paul next faces a problem which he knows could be posed. Christ's death and resurrection are proclaimed as what we might call happening literally. He really did die and was buried, and in that same body he rose from the dead. But Christians have not yet died and risen in this same bodily way. So in what way can it be said that they have already died and risen? The answer lies in that it is a death to an old way of life enmeshed in sin, and it is resurrection to a new way of life that leaves sin behind. Paul even calls our death to sin a crucifixion.

"We know that our old self was crucified with him, so that our sinful body might be done away with." But a resurrection also follows this. "If, then, we have died with Christ, we believe that we shall also live with him." We could certainly call all this Pasch as passage. In this case, Paul underlines that it is a moral passage from a sinful way of life to another whole new way. This moral passage of the Christian is rooted in Christ's own passage: "As to his death, he died to sin once and for all; as to his life, he lives for God. Consequently [and with this word Paul explains how our baptism corresponds to this], you too must think of yourselves as being dead to sin and living for God in Christ Jesus."

In the context of this Vigil liturgy, this is intense and clear theological teaching that depicts vividly what our own share in Christ's Pasch is to look like and the means by which it comes about. Only one moment will stand between what Paul says here and the third major part of the Vigil, the baptismal liturgy. That moment is the climax of this long Liturgy of the Word, the proclamation of the resurrection gospel. We turn to that now.

Alleluia, Alleluia, Alleluia

"Alleluia"—the paschal song *par excellence*—has not been sung by the church since Lent began. Now it rises up anew in this night. The priest solemnly intones it three times, each time raising his voice a step, and the assembly repeats. Then the cantor sings some of the verses of Psalm 118—the paschal psalm *par excellence*—and the assembly intervenes three times repeating a triple alleluia. All are standing, and incense surrounds the Book of the Gospels. This is the atmosphere in which we hear the Lord's resurrection proclaimed. And such a proclamation is for us nothing less than the means by which the risen Lord renders himself vividly present in our midst. At the Vigil one of the Synoptic accounts of resurrection is read, according to the three-year Lectionary cycle. I will comment briefly on each of those passages here, noting particularly what is unique in each of the evangelist's accounts and commenting especially on how the passage in question comes alive within the liturgical context. A different style is required of our commentary now. Joy, wonder, perplexity, amazement, and faith combine and are not entirely within our control. In fact, they are not within our control at all.

Once again, we should be mindful of the whole context in which this resurrection gospel is proclaimed. It is the climax of the long Liturgy of the Word. This context urges us to conclude that the entire creation and the entire action of the living God in all ages have as their goal the resurrection of the Son. Creation was for exodus, and exodus is for resurrection. This is the form of the Liturgy of the Word. And the resurrection of the Son has as its goal our share in his divine sonship and our participation in the life of the Holy Trinity. This is the form of the liturgies of baptism and Eucharist that follow.

Matthew's Account (28:1-10)

In the *Exsultet* we heard the words, "O truly blessed night, when things of heaven are wed to those of earth and divine to the human." We remember this line as we hear Matthew's account, for it features very vividly an unexpected appearance of an angel descending from heaven. As we ponder this appearance, I think it can be interesting to wonder if angels, individual angels, have the equivalent to what we would call in human beings a personality. I mean the characteristics of a particular angel, the angel's traits and style. If so, the angel in this gospel passage could be called the noisy type, even rambunctious and flashy. His arrival is accompanied by an earthquake. He rolls back the stone from the tomb. That wouldn't have been quiet. One can imagine a rumbling. His appearance is like lightning. He scares the guards and knocks them dead, and they were supposed to be guarding a dead man. Now who's dead? Then he sits on the stone he rolled back. Really? An incorporeal being bothering to sit! Is he being funny? And after all this he has the cheek to ask the women, "Did I scare you?" And then he calmly tells them not to be afraid. What do all these angelic moves mean? It is certainly a style. It creates its own kind of impression. In part it is certainly about a great tide of joy we find in many of the gospel stories of resurrection appearances. We are allowed to smile and to enjoy the details.

But we need to be clear: none of this noise and commotion comes from the resurrection itself. It is all the commotion of an angel designed to reveal an empty tomb—noise and commotion to reveal that there is no one here and no one to see. Noise and commotion to reveal what made no noise and what took place in deepest night in a manner known to God alone, with a swift, spiritual, silent stroke of transformation: the resurrection of Jesus from the dead. "Let there be light," said God into the chaos of the tomb, and there was light.

After the noisy arrival and display, the angel bids the two women who had come to the tomb not to be afraid, and then declares the meaning of the empty tomb he reveals. He refers to Jesus by a beautiful title. He calls him "Jesus the crucified." And then he announces that Jesus is not here in the tomb where he had been laid, for he has been raised. He has been raised, but his name will always be "Jesus the crucified," for never can we forget the love displayed through the long hours of his dying. And now God the Father confirms that act of love, accepts it, fixes it forever, and establishes the Crucified permanently in glory. He is the Lamb once slain who dies no more and lives forever as Jesus the Crucified, Lord and Messiah.

The angel asks the women to believe his announcement and to pass it on to the disciples of Jesus. He tells them they will see Jesus in Galilee. This is odd when we think about it. If he is risen, why should he not show himself here and now? And why Galilee? That's a long way away. Is that where he is? There and not here? If so, what does "risen" mean anyway? What does "he is not here" mean?

We can watch carefully how the women react. We hear "they went away quickly from the tomb, fearful yet overjoyed." Two lessons here: (1) move away quickly from the tomb, from the place of death; and (2) believe the angel, even if it frightens and puzzles, for there is joy for those who put their trust in the announcement. The women were running to do what the angel told them to do, "to announce this to the disciples." But then what happens? Suddenly Jesus himself meets them and greets them with a huge and simple word. "Rejoice," he says to them (my translation). The angel had told them they would see him in Galilee, but he stands before them here and now? Was the angel wrong? How here? Why now? Because they were moving away from the tomb, because they had believed the angel, because they were in mission to announce this to others—for all these reasons he appears to them here and now.

This is how we too will meet Jesus the Crucified as the Risen One: by running away from the tomb of sin and death, by believing the angel's announcement, and in mission to carry this news to others. On the way, in the mission, the women met him. Jesus shows himself suddenly how and where he will. And in his own sovereign way he will reveal himself to each of us and to all. He will come to us as we hurry away from the tomb and run to share the news with others.

Baptism and the Eucharist are the visible signs of this invisible mystery, the mystery of encounter with "Jesus the crucified . . . [who] has been raised just as he said." Like the women when they encountered him, in the Eucharist we approach him, we embrace his feet, and we do him homage.

Mark's Account (16:1-7)

Although Mark's account of resurrection is similar in some ways to Matthew's, the differences are also striking. In the liturgy itself we are not inclined to notice those differences because we hear only one account in one particular year, and that account sets its own particular tone. In the context of this present study, however, where we are looking at the various ways that Scripture used in the liturgy reveals to us the mystery of resurrection, it is worth our effort to try to make some theological sense of the differences. This will be our task as well when we look also at Luke's and John's narrations.

It is not possible to coordinate the resurrection accounts of the four evangelists. They are not consistent in their details. They create different moods. They evoke different reactions. They raise and answer theological questions differently and leave other questions unanswered. At first glance this may seem disturbing, even cause for doubt. But actually the fact that such a coordination is impossible is rooted in the new reality itself of resurrection. The texts refuse to let themselves be tamed into a simple narrative of just another something that happened and can be told. We are in a new realm now where language and narration struggle, and the different narrative styles and details of the evangelists are Spirit-inspired means that put us into contact with this new reality, this new realm of inexhaustible richness, a reality at one and the same time utterly intense and elusive and mysterious.

In Mark's account three women are making their way to the tomb, bringing spices so that they might go and anoint the body of Jesus. This intention to anoint was not mentioned at all by Matthew. Mark tells us that as the women are making their way to the tomb, they are wondering among themselves who will roll back the stone from the entrance of the tomb so that they might enter. But no flashy angel does this for them, as in Matthew, and there is no mention of an earthquake here. Rather, as Mark tells it, when the women reach the tomb, they simply see that the stone had already been rolled back. We are told that they entered the tomb. This detail was not mentioned by Matthew. It should catch our attention. We should linger on it and imagine it. It is no small matter for them to step inside the tomb where they are expecting to find the bloodied and tortured corpse of their beloved rabbi. We are moved by their courage and touched by their love. Yet they do not find at all what they were expecting to find. Rather than the corpse of the dead man, they see instead a "young man"—not an angel—who is seated "on the right side" of the tomb and "clothed in a white robe." The women are "utterly amazed." The Greek verb that describes their reaction is strong and vivid, carrying a nuance of nearly being out of one's senses, a kind of complete astonishment, something altogether new for them. We are meant to notice their reaction; Matthew did not mention it.

In Mark's telling the women are inside the tomb. The body of Jesus is not there. Instead, there is a young man dressed in white sitting in a precisely designated place. His posture and placement seem somehow to suggest calm and control, while the women for their part are on the verge of losing their control. The young man then tries to calm them with his words. He tells them not to be amazed. He tells them he knows what they are looking for. "You seek Jesus of Nazareth, the crucified." This is the same beautiful title for Jesus that Matthew's angel uttered. Next in Mark the young man announces that the Crucified "has been raised; he is not here. Behold the place where they laid him." This too is beautiful. The scene is drawn with little detail, but the announcement is crisp, clear, fresh. Three things: Jesus has been raised; he is not here in the tomb; the place where his dead body laid should be observed carefully and in wonderment.

The women are next entrusted with a commission. The young man tells them, "[G]o and tell his disciples and Peter, 'He is going before you to Galilee; there you will see him, as he told you.'" This is not unlike the message that Matthew's angel entrusted to the women. The difference is that Mark specifies "his disciples and Peter," and the young man, after mentioning seeing the risen Lord in Galilee, adds the phrase "as he told you." In the liturgy of the Vigil, this gospel passage finishes here. But to careful readers of the whole of Mark's gospel, the decision of the Lectionary to cut the passage at this point comes close to being a failure to deliver Mark's whole meaning. For in fact the next verse of the gospel is disconcerting and challenging in the extreme. It continues to keep the reader focused on the women's astonishment. How do the women respond to the young man's message? We read, "Then they went out and fled from the tomb, seized with trembling and bewilderment. They said nothing to anyone, for they were afraid" (Mark 16:8). The whole gospel ends with this verse.

Perhaps the fashioners of the Lectionary did not include it precisely because it is so difficult to explain. They would not be the first to want to avoid this problem. In fact, ancient manuscript traditions of the Gospel of Mark show that there are two different endings to it, one that ends with this disconcerting report of the women's failure to act on their commission and another longer one, clearly written by another hand, that attempts to rectify this challenging and blunt finish. Studying this situation and offering explanations of it have occupied Scripture scholars for a long time, but there is no ultimate resolution, only a range of plausible theories. This is a very vivid example of what I said about resurrection gospel narratives refusing to let themselves be tamed into a single coordinated narrative. Even so, I would like to offer one possible meditation on the mystery of resurrection that this shorter, blunt ending of Mark's Gospel suggests to me.

Because this ending is so disconcerting, it brings each of us who hear it proclaimed into a crucial dimension of the mystery of resurrection. I too must decide what I will do when faced with the testimony of the young man dressed in white. He has declared to me three things: Jesus has been raised; he is not here in the tomb; the place where his dead body had lain should be observed carefully and in wonderment. If I choose not to believe, my contact with the main point of the whole story of Jesus is over. He can be of no ultimate significance for me. If I believe, then a whole new relationship with him begins. He becomes for me the Crucified who is risen and whom I will meet elsewhere, away from this tomb, even as he said. What the rest of such a story holds for me and for every believer cannot even be attempted by the evangelist. It is as open ended and as variable and as astonishing and as stupendous as the stories of millions of believers who have trusted in the message and so come into mysterious contact with Jesus the Crucified and Risen One. It is to belief like this that Mark's abrupt ending of the gospel invites. Like the women, we have every right to be "utterly amazed" and afraid when we find in the place of death the completely unexpected announcement of life. The gospel does not tell us how the women's story finished, but it cannot have ended there. Otherwise, how would what they experienced and their reaction to it ever be known? Eventually too, they told; they bore witness to the empty tomb, to the mysterious explainer of its meaning, and to their dumbfounded first reaction.

Luke's Account (24:1-12)

The passage from Luke's gospel for the Vigil liturgy is a sophisticated interweaving of a number of scenes around the tomb and stories of appearances of the risen Lord. But it does not include an appearance. Like Matthew and Mark we have the scene of women at the tomb, but the story is told with details and a voice that create a considerably different mood and impact.

We can understand the passage better if we take note of the several verses in the previous chapter of Luke's gospel that describe the burial of Jesus. There is a strong emphasis there on the "body of Jesus." Joseph of Arimathea asks Pilate "for the body of Jesus" (Luke 23:52). Then, "After he had taken the body down, he wrapped it in a linen cloth and laid him in a rock-hewn tomb. . ." (v. 53). After this, we encounter the same women who will be mentioned at the opening of the passage read at the Vigil. We are told that "they had seen the tomb and the way in which the body was laid in it" (v. 55). They left the tomb "and prepared spices and perfumed oils" (v. 56) for the body and to observe the Sabbath rest. The passage read at the Vigil picks up from here.

These same women make their way to the tomb and to the body of Jesus that they had so carefully observed. With much less attention than Matthew or Mark give it, Luke tells us almost casually that "[t]hey found the stone rolled away from the tomb" and so simply went in. He says, "when they entered [the tomb], they did not find the body of the Lord Jesus." But at this point we are struck by the evangelist's expression in mentioning yet again the body of Jesus. Now the language about the body has changed, and it is because the narrator knows more than the women do in this moment. The narrator knows that the body the women are looking for has been raised up, and he cannot refrain from referring to it with a term expressing reverence and suggesting Jesus' glorification. It is "the body of the *Lord* Jesus."

The women had carefully observed the tomb of Jesus and how the body had been laid in it. Now they are in the tomb and the body is not to be found. "While they were puzzling over this, behold, two men in dazzling garments appeared to them." This is different from Matthew and Mark. In Matthew we saw one angel outside the tomb, seated on the stone. In Mark a young man is seen as soon as the women enter. Now in Luke the scene begins with no one present and the body of Jesus gone, and then suddenly—"behold"—two men in dazzling garments are standing beside them. Where did they come from? How did they get there? The mood and atmosphere are suddenly changed. We read that the women "were terrified and bowed their faces to the ground." These two men elicit fear and reverence. Whence their dazzling garments? Is it because of the message that they next announce? The two men speak, and their language is lofty and elegant, different from what the angel or young man had said in Matthew and Mark. They say—it is odd that they are both said to be speaking —"Why do you seek the living one among the dead? He is not here, but he has been raised." This is magnificent. Jesus is referred to by a new title. He is the Living One. And as such, if the women expect to find him in a tomb, they are completely in the wrong place. The Living One cannot be found among the dead. The dead are, of course, completely dead. One cannot be just kind of dead or a little dead. The title Living One contrasts that absolute condition of death with an absolute condition of life. Jesus can now be characterized as Life itself, all alive. He obviously is not the Living One in the sense that anything alive could be called living. No, he is the Living One in some new and definitive way. One senses in this title that death can never more be known by him. He will never be found among the dead. The two men continue their speech by reminding the women that Jesus had predicted all this when they were in Galilee, and at this reminder we are told that the women "remembered his words." Some understanding is beginning to dawn.

From here Luke passes to another scene. We are told next that the women "returned from the tomb and announced all these things to the eleven and to all the others." Here Luke mentions the names of three women who experienced this but also refers to an unspecified number of other women who had been at the tomb and who told the same story to the apostles. To those who heard the women's story, "their story seemed like nonsense and they did not believe them."

We should pause to feel the force of this scene that Luke creates with only a few carefully placed sentences. Several women are returning to a place where the eleven are gathered with other disciples. The women relate what they experienced. So far there has been no appearance of the risen Lord himself. We have only the tomb with no body of Jesus in it, men in dazzling garments with a dazzling message. The women faithfully recount what happened to them, and we do not know for sure their level of understanding or belief. We are told that the apostles do not believe.

Even so, one more scene is quickly placed before us. Peter gets up and runs to the tomb, bends down to look in, and "saw the burial cloths alone." This is very odd. The body that was laid in the tomb is not there, but the burial clothes that were wrapped around his body are. What could this mean? He must be pondering the words that the women relayed from the two men. "Why do you seek the living one among the dead? . . . Remember what he said to you while he was still in Galilee." This brief scene closes with the words, "then he [Peter] went home amazed at what had happened."

By this point in the story much has happened, but there is still no certainty about what explains it. This uncertainty will be cleared up by further stories that follow in Luke's gospel, but for the moment, at the Vigil, this is all we hear. The uncertainty of all the players in these scenes mirrors our own. We too can come to resurrection only by means of the testimony of others. The tomb is empty. What does it mean? Messengers have told us. What will we believe?

Third Part: Baptismal Liturgy

After a homily, the third part of the Vigil liturgy begins: the baptismal liturgy. The long Liturgy of the Word that announces resurrection requires a response from those who hear it. It invites to place faith in the announcement. Each person in the assembly is invited to believe that Jesus the Crucified has been raised. Each one is invited to believe in the Living One who cannot be sought among the dead. Each person is invited to encounter the body of the Lord Jesus in the new and unexpected forms in which it will manifest itself. Baptism is the expression of that act of faith. And after that expression, the person professing that faith is immediately plunged into communion in the death and resurrection of Jesus. That is to say, God immediately responds to my act of faith by splicing me into the glorified body of the Lord Jesus.

In actual fact most of the people participating in the Vigil liturgy have already been baptized. Nonetheless, at many Vigil celebrations some new members are baptized, and all the baptized renew their baptismal act of faith. The Vigil liturgy is a kind of original context for baptism, a context that reveals its deepest sense and fullest meaning for all the baptized. This remains true even though baptism is often celebrated in other settings outside this context. The Vigil context shows that baptism is not some free-floating rite that simply gets a person's Christian life underway. Rather, baptism is a turning point in our encounter with the message of Jesus' resurrection. It is the sacrament of our faith in that message. It is our communion in the new life that our risen Lord wishes to share with us. It is, as we said, in the commentary on the passage from the Letter to the Romans read in the Vigil, a ritual likeness of his death and a ritual likeness of his resurrection which accomplishes in us the very reality of which it is a likeness. It is in us "death to sin and life for God."

Fourth Part: The Liturgy of the Eucharist

Furthermore, baptism is the door through which we pass to an even more intense encounter with our risen Lord—namely, encountering him in his eucharistic Body, which is coextensive with the body of the Crucified and that body now raised up. It is communion in the Body of the Lord Jesus. This is why in the Vigil the Liturgy of the Eucharist follows immediately upon the liturgy of baptism. The newly baptized come to Eucharist for a first time. Baptism happens only once to a person. But coming to Eucharist is a regular encounter with the body of the Lord Jesus.

Within the scope of this book it is not possible to comment at any length on the liturgies of baptism, confirmation, and Eucharist that form successive climaxes of the Vigil Mass. A great deal of useful writing comments on these liturgies. For my part, I would just like to invite my reader to consider it in the context I am underlining here. Our topic here is cross and resurrection as these can be understood in the liturgies of the Triduum. Baptism and Eucharist celebrated in the Vigil liturgy show us ultimately that cross and resurrection are understood only by means of our profound participation in the same. This participation is achieved not primarily by our own efforts, though it does require our act of faith. But it is ultimately God's work and God's gift to us as God acts through the sacraments. Baptism and Eucharist are where Christ's prayer is answered, his prayer that all those who will believe in him through his disciples' preaching may be one with him in the glory of the Father.

Resurrection is not an event over and done with. It is God's deed, and it perdures. Resurrection happens in the awesome glory of this holy night. This is the night in which Christ breaks the prison bars of death. This is the night in which believers throughout the world rise up together with Christ as he leads them from the gloom of sin and joins them to his holy ones.

Chapter 8

The Mass during the Day
and the Octave of Easter

I t is clear that the Paschal Vigil is an exciting and intense point of
arrival and celebration—a point of arrival for the Triduum, for the
season of Lent, and indeed for the whole liturgical year. Reflecting
on the Vigil has given us the opportunity to discuss many dimensions
of the resurrection mystery. Yet the theme is hardly exhausted, either
in the liturgy itself or in what there is to ponder of it. The Vigil opens
outward into other liturgies of Easter day. Easter day is celebrated
for an octave of eight days. The celebration continues through forty
days until Ascension. Ascension opens a period of waiting for the
promised gift of the Holy Spirit at Pentecost. Pentecost is the climax
and ultimate point of arrival of this whole Paschal Mystery. Starting
from the Vigil and carrying on through fifty days until Pentecost, the
church's liturgy inserts us deep inside the resurrection mystery by
means of various celebrations. In what follows we will look briefly
at the way the church's liturgy arranges our exposure to Scripture
throughout these fifty days. This will give us still more opportunity
to develop and deepen our understanding. We begin with the Mass
of Easter day and follow that by looking at the Octave.

The Mass of Easter Day

From the Acts of the Apostles

The first reading at the Mass on Easter day is a brief passage of the
preaching of Peter in the Acts of the Apostles (Acts 10:34-43). It can
appear deceptively short and simple, but in fact it is a foundational

text within Acts, in that it is representative of a pattern of preaching that occurs at seven other points in that book. All the other passages in Acts where such preaching occurs will in fact be read at Masses in the days of the Octave or later within the Easter season. My comments here can serve to help us reflect on all those instances where these passages are placed in the liturgy.

What we have here in all these texts is the primitive core of the message that Peter and the other apostles began to preach so forcefully beginning on the day of Pentecost. That core, repeated in eight variations (Acts 2:22-24, 32, 36; 3:13-15; 4:10; 5:30-32; 10:39-41; 13:27-33), is an announcement of Jesus' being put to death and God raising him up. It is structured antithetically, putting in opposition human action and divine action in regard to Jesus. Responsibility for the death of Jesus is assigned to all who hear the proclamation in a phrase that basically says, "You crucified him" (slightly varied in the different passages) or, as in the text from the Easter day liturgy, "They put him to death by hanging him on a tree." Antithetical to this action of putting Jesus to death is what God instead is proclaimed to have done: "this man God raised on the third day." In four of the eight texts another basic phrase is added to the primitive core, claiming, "and we are his witnesses." That phrase is beautifully expanded in the passage read on Easter day, where Peter refers to himself and others as "witnesses chosen by God in advance, who ate and drank with him after he rose from the dead."

What all these passages show us is something that I have emphasized throughout this book. If the apostles witness to resurrection, they do not separate their witness from proclamation of his death. Indeed, the proclamation of Jesus' death includes an assignment of responsibility for it to the hearers of the proclamation. At the same time, the announcement of God's counteraction of raising Jesus from the dead makes it possible to bear this responsibility because, as the core is expanded in various forms, the resurrection of Jesus offers forgiveness of sins to those who believe in him. Not only that. The gift of the Spirit is promised as well, a Spirit that sanctifies and bestows the mission of announcing that God has raised the crucified Jesus. All this is seen in the reaction to Peter's first preaching of this core on the day of Pentecost. In reaction to it we read that his hearers "were cut to the heart, and they asked Peter and the other apostles, 'What are we to do, my brothers?' Peter said to them, 'Repent and be baptized, every one of you, in the name of Jesus Christ for the forgiveness of your sins; and you will receive the gift of the Holy Spirit.'"

The action of God in Jesus' regard has been absolute and total. Those who put him to death—ultimately all of us to whom the proclamation is addressed—had thought that it was total and absolute. But no. God's raising Jesus from the dead is what is total and absolute. For Jesus, resurrection means new life, exaltation at God's right hand, being established as Lord and Christ. For human beings, Jesus' resurrection means the remission of sins and the gift of the Holy Spirit to witness to what God has done.

How beautiful it is then at Mass on Easter morning to hear this primitive core of the message proclaimed in our midst. As we hear it, we are once again taken up into the pattern. The voice of the apostle Peter sounds clearly in our midst, and we once again are struck to the heart by what he proclaims. We recognize ourselves as among those "who believe in him [and so] will receive forgiveness of sins through his name." This is resurrection for us. And we sing of it in the responsorial psalm, Psalm 118, the paschal psalm *par excellence*. We sing, "This is the day the Lord has made; let us rejoice and be glad." That day is the day of resurrection, and it is this very day in which we are celebrating.

From the Letter to the Colossians

There is an option of one of two readings for the second reading at the day Mass. The first of these is a very short passage from the Letter to the Colossians (Col 3:1-4). It deals with our own involvement in Christ's resurrection, addressing us—the apostle's words are addressed to us—as having been "raised with Christ." A consequence follows. "If then you were raised with Christ, seek what is above, where Christ is seated at the right hand of God." The apostle gives us two reasons to seek the things that are above: first, because we have been raised with Christ; second, because Christ is "above," seated at the Father's right hand. The proclamation here is focused on Christ's resurrection and glorification as it affects us. Baptism is implicitly referred to. That is where we have been raised with Christ. But the moral conversion that baptism requires and makes possible is also at issue. This is why we are urged to seek what is above. And the point is repeated a second time, where Paul says, "Think of what is above, not of what is on earth." And then baptism is implicitly referenced again when Paul says, "For you have died, and your life is hidden with Christ in God." Baptism is a ritual death as well as ritual resurrection, but it has its consequences in our minds and hearts, and it establishes us in a particular relationship with Christ.

Paul's sense of mystery stands behind the concept here. Earlier in the book we spoke of this sense of *mystery* in Paul's thought (pp. 31–32). Christ himself is hidden, and we are hidden in him. He will come again in glory and appear. When he appears, what theretofore was hidden—that our lives already now are in him, raised with him, with him at the right hand of God—will become manifest. This will be demonstrated even now in our seeking the things above.

From the First Letter to the Corinthians

A different option for the second reading is from the First Letter to the Corinthians (5:6b-8), also a brief passage. Paul alludes to the unleavened bread used by Israel in the Passover meal and uses it as a metaphor for the moral conversion that life in Christ implies. He directly calls Christ our Pasch and declares that he has been sacrificed. This is the new Pasch that we are celebrating. And he suggests that we do it not with "the yeast of malice and wickedness, but with the unleavened bread of sincerity and truth." The phrase "Christ our Pasch has been sacrificed" is frequently quoted in the chants of the season and is found in all five of the Easter prefaces.

The Gospel according to John

We have seen that the resurrection account read at the Vigil Mass is from Matthew, Mark, or Luke. At the day Mass the gospel reading comes from the opening verses of chapter 20 of John, the beginning of yet a different set of resurrection stories, quite unlike those of the Synoptic evangelists. It creates a different mood and offers us a different direction to take our reflections.

After the long and joyous celebration of the Vigil, on Easter morning the church is standing in the full joy of the resurrection. Yet this gospel as it stands is, I think, disconcerting; for it is puzzling, inconclusive, and at first glance at least, disappointingly insignificant. Its depths unfold, however, and its meaning begins to open more and more precisely inside the liturgical celebration, on this very day of our feast, poised as the community is to celebrate the Eucharist in the liturgy that will follow. A different style of commentary is required of us now.

When we look more closely at the text we see a complex, formal ritual that guides the movements of three disciples at an open tomb. Everyone is running: Mary of Magdala running away from the tomb, two other disciples racing each other toward the tomb. The movements of the three are a dance circling an open center, a hole cut into the earth, a tomb. Each dancer moves differently, but the choreography the dancers follow unfolds into a single pattern revealing a completely unexpected and totally new truth.

Let us observe more closely the details of each, watching how each one's movements come together to form the whole. Mary of Magdala arrives at the tomb, the evangelist pointedly tells us, "while it was still dark." Thus we know that whatever happened there had happened in the night, the same night during which we kept vigil perhaps some twelve hours or more ago. She observed "the stone removed from the tomb." For the careful listener, this phrase begins to vibrate with mysterious echoes that are clues to its full significance. One of these evokes Jesus' encounter with another woman, the Samaritan woman at the well of Jacob. She had said to him, "Sir, you do not even have a bucket and the cistern is deep; where then can you get this living water?" (John 4:11). The echo says, "The tomb is deep and a corpse lies wrapped and sealed within; what life can be expected here in this dark domain of death?" And yet unexpectedly, the stone is already removed from the tomb when Mary arrives, just as Jacob, Jesus' ancestor and foreshadowing, had once rolled the stone from the mouth of a well so that Rachel could water her flocks (Gen 29:10). As the Samaritan woman had run off to tell the people of the village about the man she had met at the well, Mary runs off to tell the disciples that she has found an open tomb. The tomb is to become a spring of life-giving water.

Enter now two other dancers, Peter and the disciple whom Jesus loved. Peter, already established as the head of the band of disciples that Jesus had formed, sets out immediately toward the tomb. The other disciple, who represents loving intimacy with Jesus, enters the dance in the same direction but with faster step. Here we see in elementary shape two essential ingredients of the about-to-be-formed church: external office in the authority of Peter together with interior, intimate love. They run side by side toward the dark and mysterious sign. Love arrives first but waits for the external authority to enter.

Now the dance slows. The movements grow more deliberate. Yet their precise meaning escapes us, as it escapes the dancers themselves. Nonetheless, we keep our eyes fixed on what they see, as they also do; and slowly, slowly it is not understanding that emerges but something that overwhelms and surpasses understanding, all the while planting itself more firmly in their experience and ours. The evangelist is clear about this. He says, "For they did not yet understand the Scripture that he had to rise from the dead." So what is it, then, that happens there? What is the experience?

We regard closely the one disciple on whom the dance is concentrated now, the disciple whom Jesus loved. He stops outside the tomb but bends down and looks in. He sees the burial clothes there, but there is no understanding. He waits and lets Peter go in before him. Now we see him standing still outside the tomb—beside the well, we could say. He has no bucket, and the well is deep. A hole opens in the rock into the center of the earth, all the way to death. In this still moment, suspense carried to the breaking point, another echo is heard: the words of the Lord God to Moses, who had asked—audaciously—to see God's face. And God answered him, "Here is a place near me where you shall station yourself on the rock. When my glory passes I will set you in the hollow of the rock and will cover you with my hand until I have passed by. Then I will remove my hand, so that you may see my back; but my face in not to be seen" (Exod 33:21-23). Now at the tomb the beloved disciple steps into the cleft of the rock, and the glory of the Lord flashes by. He does not see his face. We are told simply, "he saw and believed." But what did he see? What did he believe? For we are told immediately after, "they did not yet understand the Scripture that he had to rise from the dead."

The evangelist is telling us that love has entered the tomb and something is quickened within him. It is an interior gasp in which he is the first to *experience* or *sense* the resurrection—not to understand it, but to feel it moving within him and to detect the movement with his belief. Now the dance is completely stilled, and the only movement is within. Inside that tomb is the still point of the turning world. The world of death swirls all round. And yet on this day, in this hour, we can stand with the beloved disciple at this still point and the interior gasp of the resurrection can quicken within us also. We remember the words of Jesus, "Whoever believes in me, as Scripture says, 'Rivers of living water will flow from *within* him'" (John

7:38; emphasis mine). The well is deep, but we have been given a bucket. The place is dark, but it is the first day of the week, the first day of an entirely new creation, the day on which God said, "Let there be light" (Gen 1:3). In the darkness around the tomb a dawn begins, and the apostle Paul helps us to detect the same dimensions within us: "For God who said, 'Let light shine out of darkness,' has shown in our hearts to bring to light the knowledge of the glory of God on the face of Christ" (2 Cor 4:6).

In this dance only the eyes of the beloved disciple move now. What does he see? Discarded grave clothes, indicating that the veiled mystery is now unfurled before us. Special attention is given to "the cloth that had covered his head, . . . [neatly] rolled up in a separate place." In Greek this is *soudarion*, literally a sweat cloth, and we hear the echo of the curse of sin that we shall live "by the sweat of [our] face" (Gen 3:19). This penalty is henceforth cancelled and left behind. A *soudarion* had covered the face of Lazarus when Jesus called him forth from the tomb. On that day Jesus commanded, "Untie him and let him go" (John 11:44). On Easter this grace is extended to us all. With the beloved disciple we see discarded grave clothes, and we remember that after their fall, our first parents realized they were naked and, feeling ashamed, covered themselves (Gen 3:7). The new Adam leaves this shame behind, and cancels that penalty as well, leaving the clothes behind. He had said, "No one takes [my life] from me. . . . I have power to lay it down, and power to take it up again" (John 10:18). In the night he had taken it up again, and he leaves behind him the garments and the shame of death.

Other movements of this dance will be seen in the days ahead, in the gospel read each day of the Octave. The Octave!—a symbol in time of that never-ending Day into which the liturgies of many days will splice us. This scene is followed by Mary of Magdala actually seeing Jesus but being told, "Stop holding on to me." He says this to teach that the experience of him is interior and surpassing what can be grasped. He tells her to go and tell his brothers that he is ascending "to my Father and your Father, to my God and your God." That is, the resurrection of Jesus has bequeathed to us his very own relation to the eternal Father.

But for the moment we stand here in the tomb, in the cleft of the rock, with the beloved disciple. As we turn toward the altar on which we will celebrate the Eucharist, we grasp that the action performed there will somehow present to us anew the dance on which we have meditated. There is very little to see: a few clothes neatly folded, bread, wine, a cup. We do not see the Lord's face. But in the "cleft" of the altar around which we stand, his glory flashes by. From within us, a well of living water is quickened. Each of us is a disciple whom Jesus loves, and each of us loves him. So we see the altar, and we believe. Peter's presence and authority confirms our experience. Jesus is the Christ, the Son of the Living God. To whom else could we go? He has the words of eternal life. And in the end, as our encounters with the risen Lord continue, we shall borrow the words of Peter, who borrowed love's words, and we will say to him, "Lord, you know everything; you know that I love you" (John 21:17).

Eight Days, Forty Days, and Fifty Days

The joy of Easter and the immensity of the mystery of resurrection cannot be contained in a single day of celebration. Thus it is that the church's liturgical calendar is arranged in such a way as to extend the celebration into the following days and weeks. The first unit of time is the Octave, a set of eight days beginning on Easter Sunday and continuing to the following Sunday. These are days of liturgy in which the intensity of the Vigil and of Easter day are continued even on weekdays and as many of us return to our regular activities. Also beginning on Easter Sunday the liturgy counts forty days to the day of the Lord's Ascension. Between Ascension and Pentecost ten more days pass, and in those days the church's liturgy has us waiting and praying for the gift of the outpouring of the Holy Spirit, as Jesus instructed and promised.

During these fifty days the church's Lectionary exposes us to virtually all the key scriptural texts on resurrection—from the four gospels, the Acts of the Apostles, the book of Revelation, and many passages from the apostolic letters. The church's prayers—the antiphons, the presidential prayers, the prefaces—all deepen our participation in this marvelous mystery. Commentary on all that, as we have done especially on the Triduum and Easter day, would certainly be possible, but would be extensive. I will limit commentary here to an indication of the logic of the Lectionary for the Octave, then to the structure of the Lectionary from the Octave to Ascension. This will allow for a fuller commentary on Ascension and then Pentecost. We continue with our method of using the setting of the liturgy to help us explore the sense of the scriptural texts.

The Octave

Readings from Acts during the Octave of Easter

The first reading during each day of the Easter Octave is taken from the Acts of the Apostles. On Monday and Tuesday we hear substantial portions of Peter's long homily given on the day of Pentecost immediately after he and the other disciples had received the outpouring of the Holy Spirit. In each of these two passages we hear again some variation of what I called above the substantial core of the apostolic kerygma— namely, witnessing to the resurrection, but never separating that witness from proclamation of the Lord's death.

Wednesday's reading from Acts (3:1-10) tells the story of how Peter and John were involved in the miraculous cure of a man who had been crippled from birth. This draws the attention of all the people in the temple area. On Thursday, Friday, and Saturday we follow the story of all that developed because of this healing. Thursday's passage (Acts 3:11-26) begins with a scene beautiful to imagine: "As the crippled man who had been cured clung to Peter and John, all the people hurried in amazement toward them . . ." In this excited context, Peter—with John beside him and the cured man clinging—immediately takes advantage of the occasion to address all the people and to announce the resurrection to them. He explains that the crippled man had been cured not by some special power that he or John possessed, but by God's "servant Jesus," who again is essentially described according to the basic pattern of "you crucified him, but God raised him up."

In Friday's passage (Acts 4:1-12) this same story continues to develop. Peter and John have been arrested for stirring up the people. The next day they are brought before the religious leaders of Israel and asked to explain themselves. Once again we hear the core refrain. The crippled man was cured "in the name of Jesus Christ the Nazorean whom you crucified, whom God raised from the dead." Saturday's passage (Acts 4:13-21) continues on from this. Peter and John are released from custody and told "not to speak or teach at all in the name of Jesus." They answer, "It is impossible for us not to speak about what we have seen and heard." They have shown themselves to be fearless witnesses.

Each of these weekday passages from Acts is meant to expand day after day the church's exposure to the basic kerygmatic core that we examined in lengthier remarks about the passage from Acts read on Easter day. I repeat what the liturgy repeats: the voice of the apostle Peter sounds clearly in our midst, and we once again are struck to the heart by what he proclaims (see Acts 2:37). In his proclamation of Jesus we recognize ourselves as among "everyone who believes in him" who "will receive forgiveness of sins through his name" (Acts 10:43). This is resurrection for us, one joyful day after another.

The Gospels for the Octave Days

On each day of the Octave, the gospel passage read in the liturgy is a resurrection appearance taken from one of the four gospels. In this way the church hears virtually all the resurrection accounts that the four gospels contain. *On Monday* the passage is from Matthew's gospel (28:8-15), repeating in part and continuing on with the passage that is read in the Vigil in Year A. It tells of Jesus suddenly appearing before Mary Magdalene and the other Mary as they hurry from the tomb. Meanwhile, some of the guards at the tomb told the chief priests all that had happened, and a story is fabricated that Jesus' disciples came and stole his body in the night. One thing at least is clear from this fabrication: the body of Jesus is no longer to be found in the tomb, no matter what the explanation is.

The resurrection appearance in *Tuesday's* liturgy is taken from John's gospel (20:11-18) and creates a mood of a different sort. It is the continuation of the passage read at the Easter day Mass, which I described as three dancers circling and entering an empty tomb. Now Mary is alone at the tomb, weeping. She sees two angels inside the tomb but is oddly unmoved by their presence. She turns around and actually sees Jesus but mistakes him for a gardener. It is not until he addresses her by name that she recognizes him and exclaims, moving to embrace him. He forbids the embrace and instead commissions her to "go to my brothers [the apostles] and tell them, 'I am going to my Father and your Father, to my God and your God.'" In the liturgy this whole scene is repeated as a revelation of the way in which the Lord works mysteriously in each of us, calling each of us by name and commissioning us to announce his resurrection.

Wednesday's and Thursday's gospel passages are a further exposure to Luke's sophisticated interweaving of resurrection stories. We examined the beginning of Luke's development in the gospel passage used for Year C at the Vigil. On these weekdays of the Octave we hear, first, on Wednesday, the well-known account of the Lord's appearance, at first unrecognized, to two disciples along the road to Emmaus (Luke 24:13-35). The three speak at length as they make their way along the road. This story gives striking evidence of a theme we have touched upon at length in our reflections: the crisis that the disciples experienced at the death of Jesus. But it is the risen Jesus himself, still unrecognized, who corrects their understanding in the discussion. He rebukes them, saying, "How slow of heart to believe all that the prophets spoke! Was it not necessary that the Christ should suffer these things and enter into his glory?" Yet again we see a fundamental theme of our study repeated: cross and resurrection held in inextricable, dynamic tension, and here it is the Lord himself who explains this.

This discussion comes to an unexpected finish. They stop to eat. We read, "while he was with them at table, he took bread, said the blessing, broke it, and gave it to them. With that their eyes were opened and they recognized him, but he vanished from their sight." In this story we can recognize the pattern of every eucharistic liturgy as the context for us of a privileged and prolonged encounter with the risen Lord. In the Liturgy of the Word, the Lord is present, even if unrecognized, and the Scriptures are explained to us in such a way that we understand cross and resurrection as their central message. Then, an even greater intensity of presence is experienced in the Eucharist, in the act of Jesus saying the blessing, breaking the bread, and giving it to them. At this point Jesus vanishes, but not because he is no longer present. His presence is new, interior, deeper than ever before, not to be reduced to touch and sight, a joy and understanding that fills our minds and hearts. Like the disciples, we set out immediately to witness to others what we have experienced.

Thursday's gospel passage (Luke 24:35-48) continues this development. There is a sense of an excited sharing of different encounters with the risen Lord: Simon's encounter and the prolonged encounter of the two along the road and in the breaking of bread. In Thursday's liturgy we can sense the same excitement as we hear the words proclaimed, "While they were still speaking about this, [Jesus] stood in their midst and said to them, 'Peace be with you.'" We can enumerate the appearances we have here: (1) an appearance to Simon somewhere, no details; (2) the appearance to these two along the road; (3) now an appearance to all of them. A joyful momentum is building. In this passage the disciples are at first startled and confused. But Jesus calms them, "explains" himself to them, as it were, by showing them his hands and feet—his wounds!—and he even invites them to touch him, lest they think him some vague spirit or ghost. Even more, he eats something in their presence. This scene climaxes with the same core of the kerygma heard now from the very lips of the risen Jesus. He is said to have "opened their minds to understand the Scriptures," and he summarizes his message in these words: "Thus it is written that the Christ would suffer and rise from the dead on the third day and that repentance, for the forgiveness of sins, would be preached in his name to all the nations, beginning from Jerusalem. You are witnesses of these things." We see it yet again: death and resurrection held in inextricable union and the disciples as witnesses. Through the liturgy and the presence of the same risen Lord that we experience there, we have our minds opened to understand the Scriptures and become witnesses ourselves who continue the original apostolic witness.

Friday's gospel reading (John 21:1-14) takes us back to John's gospel and lets us experience yet a different kind of resurrection appearance that creates a different mood and spirit. Chapters 20 and 21 of John's gospel deal with four appearances of the risen Lord in a carefully arranged sequence. The church's Lectionary does not keep this sequence immediately together, though the use of them is well timed, in the Octave and ultimately on Pentecost. We have seen already the first scene of these resurrection stories in the passage read on Easter morning. This is followed by the appearance to Mary Magdalene read on Tuesday. After that in the gospel there is an appearance to the disciples hid behind locked doors on Sunday evening, then another appearance to them eight days later in the same place behind locked doors. These two appearances form the gospel passage read on the Sunday of the Octave, and we will speak of them shortly. In the gospel, the passage read on Friday of the Octave follows this, and from a literary point of view it appears as a kind of addition to the whole gospel, which already seems to conclude with the words of John 20:30-31. The appearances spoken of in chapter 20 take place in Jerusalem. The appearance in chapter 21, read on Friday, takes place at the Sea of Tiberias, in Galilee. This difference in place is in part what creates the different mood of the experience.

Of all the Lord's resurrection appearances in the four gospels, this one shows, among other things, that the risen Lord intends to come along with us in our daily lives. Yes, he is now glorious Lord. He is beyond death. He lives already the future of us all in the presence of the Father. His human body is completely suffused with divine glory. And yet, here he is with us in our normal time, in our daily living. "I am going fishing," says Peter, and six other disciples go along. They are somehow back to their normal lives in Galilee. And Jesus is there, but he appears not in the thunder and lightning of a divine being, but just as an ordinary man walking along the shore, at first unrecognized. He is an ordinary man who asks a normal question of fishermen: "[H]ave you caught anything to eat?" When they answer no, Jesus also does something normal enough, the kind of talk of people around lakes. A little advice from perhaps another fisherman: "Cast the net over the right side of the boat and you will find something." This too is a normal enough suggestion, but their following his simple advice results suddenly in a huge and unexpected sign: a catch so large that they were unable to pull the net up. It is love that is first able to recognize the meaning of the sign, and the evangelist says so explicitly: "[T]he disciple whom Jesus loved said to Peter, 'It is the Lord.'" What follows seems odd to us. Peter gets dressed and then jumps into the water. This joyfully expresses Peter's urgency to encounter Jesus again. He wishes to make himself presentable, for he was lightly clad.

John's exclamation, Peter's excitement—these are meant to be for us models of our own reactions to encountering the risen Lord. But we should not forget that in all these appearances, it is not just an important encounter for the one who sees the Lord. These are real encounters for Jesus too, who is risen in all his humanity. How pleased he must have been at John's recognition, how tenderly moved at Peter's impulsive jumping into the water.

Up to this point the scene is normal enough. Even if the catch is large and a man jumping out of the boat all of a sudden is odd, we are still in the realm of the possible. The scene continues in its ordinariness, but slowly an element of mystery seeps into the account. "When they climbed out on shore, they saw a charcoal fire with fish on it and bread." Then there is a strange invitation from the stranger: "Come, have breakfast." And, "none of the disciples dared to ask him, 'Who are you?' for they realized it was the Lord." Then he uses again those gestures that he used in the meal with them the night before he died: "Jesus came over and took the bread and gave it to them, and in like manner the fish."

When we remember that the proclamation of the gospel in the liturgy reveals the mystery of what is happening in the gathered assembly, our hearts thrill at the reading of this passage. There are seven disciples in the scene, one to represent every possible type gathered in any given assembly: the impulsive Peter, the doubting Thomas, the shrewd Nathaniel, the intense-in-their-feelings sons of Zebedee, and "two other disciples" for those who do not recognize themselves among those already named. And now us. Even though it is the Easter season and wonderful mysteries of grace are unfolding, we still must go on with our ordinary lives. "I'm going fishing." "We'll come with you." And so here we are. But wait! Suddenly, the beloved disciple's message resounds deep in our hearts: "It is the Lord!" And we realize that he is here in our very midst!

The gospel passage read on Saturday in the Octave is from Mark. We saw that the Markan passage read in the Vigil in Year B offers the earlier, abrupt ending to the gospel. The passage read on Saturday is from the so-called Longer Ending (Mark 16:9-15). It is not difficult to note in the text a different voice from that of the rest of Mark's gospel. These are verses that reflect an author with a combined knowledge of resurrection traditions that are separate from each other in the different gospels. It is like a list of those appearances loosely strung together:

- Jesus' appearance "first to Mary Magdalene" is also told in Matthew, with "another Mary" (28:8-10) and John (20:11-18).

- That Mary "told his companions . . . they did not believe" is similar to the account of Luke 24:9-11.

- Jesus' appearance in another form to two of them "walking along on their way to the country" is a very abbreviated and less theologically dense reference to the Emmaus story from Luke 24.

- Mark's comment that two disciples to whom Jesus had appeared, "returned and told the others; but they did not believe them either," is similar to the disciples' return in Luke 24:33-34, but in Luke there is no mention of disbelief; on the contrary, the returning disciples are greeted with the words, "The Lord has truly been raised and has appeared to Simon!"

- Mark's report that "later, as the Eleven were at table, he appeared to them and rebuked them for their unbelief . . ." is similar to the account of Luke 24, but the mood and tone are very different.

- Jesus' commission in Mark, "Go into the whole world and proclaim the Gospel to every creature," coincides roughly with commission scenes at the end of Luke's gospel (Luke 24:47-49) and Matthew's gospel (Matt 28:18-20).

We can sense the wisdom of the church in placing this passage from the Longer Ending of Mark's gospel toward the end of the Octave days. It is like a review of the week, and as such it is sweet and effective to hear it. The commission with which the passage ends is striking because only here is the commission to proclaim the Gospel—not to all nations, as in Matthew (28:19) and Luke (24:47), but "to every creature" (Mark 16:15). Patristic commentators noted this difference and made much of it. Jesus' resurrection affects the whole creation, and the Good News must be proclaimed not only to other human beings but to the whole creation. As the psalmist prophesied, "Let everything that has breath / give praise to the LORD!" (Ps 150:6). Or as Jesus, entering his Passion's triumphant procession into Jerusalem, exclaimed, "I tell you, if they [my disciples] keep silent, the stones will cry out!" (Luke 19:40).

Sundays feel different from weekdays for Christians, and that is as it should be. Every Sunday remembers and celebrates resurrection. And so the *Sunday in the Octave*, its eighth day, is a big day of joyful liturgy. The gospel text for that day is a strong, lengthy passage from John's gospel (20:19-31). It tells first of Jesus suddenly coming to the disciples who are gathered in hiding behind locked doors. (This appearance is also the gospel reading on Pentecost, and I will say more about it later.) Thomas was not present at this first appearance of Jesus and refuses to believe what the others tell him. About midway through the passage we hear the phrase, "Now a week later [literally "eight days later," which is an octave] his disciples were again inside and Thomas was with them." When we hear this phrase, we can register in our minds with quiet joy that this very day when we are hearing this gospel is eight days after Easter, the eighth day of the Octave. The encounter between Jesus and the doubting Thomas is somehow repeating itself now in our hearing. Jesus says to Thomas,

"Put your finger here and see my hands, and bring your hand and put it into my side, and do not be unbelieving, but believe."

There is a sense in which we easily identify with Thomas's difficulty in believing and are grateful to him somehow that his unbelief elicited this firm and tangible lesson from Jesus to bring him to belief. Thomas expressed his belief in a short, intense exclamation that has entered Christian piety as a prayer for expressing our own belief in the face of doubt: "My Lord and my God!" As we hear the story, we feel our hearts saying the same. And then we hear Jesus' next words as referring directly to ourselves. He says, "Blessed are those who have not seen and have believed."

The communion antiphon which the Missal suggests for this day has the congregation singing the following words as it approaches to receive the Lord's Body and Blood: "Bring your hand and feel the place of the nails, and do not be unbelieving but believing, alleluia." This should be a strong and intense time of prayer for us, a type of climax to this whole Octave of celebrating resurrection. We realize that it is especially by means of the Eucharist and our communion in it that we can do the very thing that Thomas did. We too can touch the Body of the Lord, the body which was crucified for us and which is now risen and present to us. We are not unbelieving, but believing. We receive him praying, "My Lord and my God!"

The Period between the Octave and the Ascension

Resurrection remains the theme day after day in the liturgy of the weeks that follow the Octave. This is true of both the weekday and Sunday lectionaries, which are arranged differently. On weekdays the first readings are taken from the Acts of the Apostles, and we hear the exciting and joyful stories of the ways the preaching and acceptance of the Good News of resurrection are spreading "in Jerusalem, throughout Judea and Samaria, and to the ends of the earth" (Acts 1:8). Gospel readings are taken from John's gospel. Although these are passages that in the gospel recount things Jesus said and did before his death and resurrection, their proclamation during the Easter season helps us hear in the words a special resonance: the mysterious foreshadowing in all that Jesus does and says of his greatest deed, his "hour," his being lifted up—on the cross, in resurrection, in ascension.

The Lectionary for the Sundays of Easter is arranged differently. During all the other Sundays of the year the first reading is always from a book of the Old Testament. During the Easter season the first reading is from Acts and the second reading from Revelation or one of the apostolic letters. The gospel for the Third Sunday of Easter in Years A, B, and C is always a different resurrection appearance. In Year A it is Luke's Emmaus appearance; in year B, the scene in Luke that immediately follows this; in Year C, John's account of the appearance by the Sea of Tiberias to the seven disciples. The Fourth Sunday of Easter is often called Good Shepherd Sunday because the gospel readings of Years A, B, and C each offer passages from chapter 10 of John's gospel, where Jesus describes himself as the Good Shepherd who lays down his life for his sheep. Again, these are words that Jesus speaks before his death and resurrection, but in the context of the Easter season they find their fullest sense.

The Fifth and Sixth Sundays of Easter in a three-year cycle offer gospel passages from chapters 13 to 15 of John's gospel. These are chapters which contain Jesus' intimate and instructive words to his disciples during the supper with them on the night before he dies. As such they are words which help us to understand the whole range of the mystery we are celebrating during these fifty days. By these intense words of Jesus we gain insight into all the dimensions of the Paschal Mystery that throughout this book we have attempted to see in their relation to each other. His words precede his death, but we hear them now in the season of resurrection. It is to both death and resurrection that his words now clearly refer. The church understands this and so does not hesitate to place these words in the liturgy after the resurrection, even if chronologically they were uttered before it. This is another indication that the liturgy does not present us with a simple historical and chronological story; Jesus' words pronounced in the intensity of a particular historical setting in fact expand beyond that immediate context and unite all the dimensions of the Paschal Mystery, before they were said and after. They refer also to a "going away" so that the Spirit can come. Here, going away does not mean an absence but a presence that will be known through the Spirit, who will "guide you [us] to all truth" (John 16:13). So on these Fifth and Sixth Sundays of Easter, and on the weekdays that follow, the church is looking toward the approaching solemnities of Ascension and Pentecost.

Chapter 9

The Ascension of the Lord

A
scension occurs on the Thursday of the Sixth Week of Easter, which is the fortieth day after Easter Sunday; or, in countries (or regions within countries) where Ascension is not observed as a holy day of obligation, it is celebrated on the Seventh Sunday of Easter. Forty days is a symbolic number, not a literal calculation. In fact, in all the scriptural passages which refer to resurrection and the ultimate glorification of Jesus, it is only in the Acts of the Apostles, in the passage that will be read in this day's liturgy, that the scheme of forty days between resurrection and ascension is laid down. In all other passages there is no precise indication of a time frame. In Luke's gospel it would seem the ascension takes place on the same single day that all the other resurrection appearances happen. In Matthew there is no ascension scene, nor in the shorter ending of Mark. The longer ending mentions it but without specifying a time. We will say more about all this as we compare the three Synoptic options for the gospel passage to be read on this day. John's gospel does not end with ascension, though the risen Lord, in the appearance to Mary Magdalene, refers to his ascending as something not yet accomplished and that he is doing even as he speaks to her (John 20:17).

What are we to make of all this? Once again we come up against a refusal of the texts to let themselves be tamed into a simple, single, consistent chronological narrative. The reality exceeds such limits because resurrection is an event both within time and that transcends time. Nonetheless, on the basis of all these texts we can say something about the resurrection-ascension nexus and the time within which all this happens. We saw that after the death of Jesus there was a period of time, not very long, in which his disciples were in extreme crisis. This is followed by another period in which the crucified Jesus "appeared in another form" to them (Mark 16:12), showing himself alive and thus vindicated by his Father. In addition to there being several appearances, in this time frame there is also some instruction from Jesus himself about the nature and meaning of his death and resurrection (Matt 28:18-20; Mark 16:14-19; Luke 24:25-27, 38-49; John 20:21-23, 27; 21:15-22). Only the text in Acts 1 specifies that this period of appearances and instruction lasted for forty days. That text and time period became deeply embedded in Christian consciousness, especially once the observance of 40 and 50 days was established in the liturgical practice of the church. This causes us to conflate in our imagination the other texts that allude to ascension or to what we quickly imagine is ascension.

Even so, all the texts agree, at least implicitly, that the period of appearances and instruction by the risen Lord comes to an end. Ultimately, it is followed by another period intimately connected with it: the coming of the Holy Spirit at Pentecost. We are still in that period now, two millennia later. The church lives in that space, that period of time, a time we can call "after Pentecost." It is a time deeply rooted in the death, resurrection, and ascension of Jesus and simultaneously transcending them all, radiating their consequences in *Spiritual* forms. So in effect the solemnity of the Ascension celebrates the ending of the period of resurrection appearances and instruction. But why would that be cause for joy? What does it mean? That is what we will seek to understand now.

A Reading from the Acts of the Apostles

In the first reading of today's liturgy from the Acts of the Apostles (1:1-11), we encounter the time scheme of forty days. The passage is from the opening verses of the entire book and refers back to what the author calls "the first book," meaning the Gospel of Luke. It is generally agreed that Luke and Acts are the work of one author, divided into two volumes. The author describes precisely the scope of the first book as dealing "with all that Jesus did and taught until the day he was taken up." That day is today's feast. And it defines the end of the period of time I indicated above. The last thing we hear about in this period is Jesus "giving instructions through the Holy Spirit to the apostles whom he had chosen."

The following verses expand on this last point, offering more details than "the first book" about the nature and purpose of this period. During it Jesus "presented himself alive to them [his disciples] by many proofs after he had suffered, appearing to them during forty days and speaking about the kingdom of God." We have already examined the stories of appearances from the different gospels, and not all such appearances are recounted in the gospels (cf. Luke 24:34; John 20:30-31; 21:25; 1 Cor 15:5-7). But it is lovely and alluring also to wonder about the content of the "speaking about the kingdom of God." What believer would not want to know what the risen Lord might say in his own words about the kingdom of God? We have only a few indications in the four gospels (Matt 28:18-20; Mark 16:14-18; Luke 24:25-27, 44-49; John 20:21-23). They are, of course, precious to us and have been much pondered through the centuries. A few verses here in Acts add a little more to that comparatively slim content. But perhaps we would not be wrong to think that some of the risen Jesus' "speaking about the kingdom of God" with his disciples shows up in the way the apostles preach and act in the Acts of the Apostles. This would mean that the amazing preaching of Peter on the day of Pentecost and after is prepared for by this period of instruction by the risen Lord himself. Here Holy Spirit and risen Jesus closely coincide. Peter and all the apostles speak and act under the influence of both.

One of the details that the present passage from Acts adds to the content of Jesus' resurrection teaching is his enjoining his disciples "not to depart from Jerusalem." His very words are cited. He says, "[W]ait for 'the promise of the Father about which you have heard me speak; for . . . in a few days you will be baptized with the Holy Spirit.'" All this is talk about the kingdom of God. The gift of the Holy Spirit coincides with the kingdom, as does Jesus' own resurrection and ascension. The kingdom is being definitively established in and through him, with his crucified and risen body as radiant center of emanation.

The scene shows us that during this period the disciples are able to ask the risen Lord questions. Here they ask, "Lord, are you at this time going to restore the kingdom to Israel?" This question is deflected by Jesus, not answered directly; but it is certainly answered, and the answer is centered on two words: *power* and *witnesses*. Jesus says, "It is not for you to know the time or seasons that the Father has established by his own authority. But you will receive *power* when the

Holy Spirit comes upon you, and you will be my *witnesses* in Jerusalem, throughout Judea and Samaria, and to the ends of the earth" (emphasis mine). To receive the *power* of the Holy Spirit and to be commissioned as *witnesses*—this is the kingdom of God among us. The geographical scheme indicates the movement from Jesus as radiant center in Jerusalem emanating through his appointed witnesses to the ends of the earth. So, back to the question that provoked this answer: "Lord, are you at this time going to restore the kingdom to Israel?" The deflected answer explained would be: yes, now in their being given the power of the Holy Spirit and made witnesses; no, in that there is still more than that to come.

Next we read, "When he had said this, as they were looking on, he was lifted up, and a cloud took him from their sight." In the liturgical tradition and in theology, we refer to this as "ascension," even though, strictly speaking, that term is never used in any of the scriptural texts. (But see John 20:17.) All the verb forms describing it are in the passive voice. He "was taken," "was lifted up," "was separated," "was carried up." In the passage from Acts, more details are given than can be found in the several other gospel texts that refer to something like this scene. Notably, words having to do with seeing and not seeing are insistently repeated. This is a clue to understanding the point that Luke wants to make. We have just seen the phrase "as they were looking on." With this, it is said that Jesus is taken "from their sight" (literally, "from their eyes"). Then Luke tells us "they were looking intently at the sky as he was going," a third mention of looking. And then "suddenly two men dressed in white garments stood beside them. They said, 'Men of Galilee, why are you standing there looking at the sky?'" This is the fourth mention of looking. Two men suddenly standing there in white garments is very similar in language and content to the two men that suddenly appeared to the women inside the tomb in Luke's account of the women at the tomb (Luke 24:4). Note, they are not said to be angels, as Christian iconography often depicts them.

Their question—"why are you looking up?"—may strike us as a reproach. I instinctively want to ask, "What's wrong with looking up? Wouldn't you?" Actually, there's nothing wrong with it. Their question in fact is establishing a point, a point that contains a promise. The point is understood by catching allusions deep inside the biblical world.

In the background of this language, we are to recognize an intimation of a scene between the disciple Elisha and his master Elijah (2 Kgs 2:9-12). As Elijah was preparing to depart from him, Elisha asked him for the gift of a double portion of his spirit. Elijah tells him that if he *sees* him being carried off to heaven, then his request will be granted. This is surely why looking intently is emphasized so strongly here. The disciples do indeed *see* Jesus being taken. The two men confirm that they have indeed seen him. They further add, "This Jesus who has been taken up from you into heaven will return in the same way as you have seen him going into heaven." This is the fifth mention of seeing. Now a new and future seeing is promised, a seeing intimately connected to their having seen him taken up. The gift of the Spirit is implied and guaranteed in the fact of their seeing. As Elisha saw Elijah taken up and so was given a share of his spirit, so now the disciples, looking so intently, see Jesus taken up and are guaranteed a share in his Holy Spirit. As Elijah is expected to return in the same fiery chariot in which he was seen carried to heaven, so Jesus is expected to be seen again "in the same way you have seen him going into heaven." (See also Dan 7:13, which in other texts is the basis for the image of Jesus' future return as the Son of Man. See Matt 24:30; 26:64; Mark 13:26; 14:62; Luke 21:27; Rev 14:14.)

Recall that in Luke's account of the transfiguration, two men identified as Moses and Elijah are said to have "appeared in glory" with Jesus. Only in Luke do we hear specified that Moses and Elijah "spoke [with Jesus] of his exodus he was going to accomplish in Jerusalem" (Luke 9:31). And who better than Moses and Elijah to speak with Jesus about the ways that the deepest meaning of so many events *they* lived or words *they* spoke in fact referred to him? (See Luke 24:26 and 24:44.) We would not be too far afield to suspect that in Luke's mind, it is the very Moses and Elijah, the two men who stood with Jesus at his transfiguration, who also stood in the tomb on Easter morning *and* who stood beside the disciples as they intently watched Jesus' own exodus, his being taken up into glory. "Why do you seek the living one among the dead?" the two men in the tomb asked (Luke 24:5). "Why are you standing there looking at the sky?" they ask now. The kingdom of God is pressing in on the disciples from every direction and with glory.

The two men speak of Jesus "taken up from you into heaven." Ordinarily, such wording would seem to suggest Jesus' absence.

But does being "taken up from you into heaven" mean he has gone elsewhere, that he is no longer here? No. It is a new form of his presence to us. In his glorified state, he has become the One who comes. He "will return in the same way." Now he has become the one who is always coming. This is seen also in the book of Revelation, where the Lord makes his presence felt, reveals himself, and says, "I am . . . the one who is and who was and who is to come, the almighty" (Rev 1:8). Ascension is a feast in which we too still experience this new form of his presence, at once more pervasive and more elusive than a single locatable, talk-to-him, see-him, touch-his-wounds presence.

The Gospel Readings for Ascension

The first reading from Acts is somehow the dominant narrative event of this liturgy on this day. The text is too rich in detail and too compelling to be otherwise. More usually the narrations of Scripture in the liturgy climax in the gospel text. On Ascension the Lectionary offers a different gospel for Years A, B, and C, while every year the first reading is the same text from Acts. This first reading inevitably impacts the way we experience the gospel text. This is all to the good, but the effect is richer if we take account, first, of notable differences that we find in each Synoptic text as well as differences in all of them from what we have just examined in Acts. None of the gospel texts is located within a time scheme of forty days, even though within this liturgy we inevitably tend to hear them that way.

In Year A the gospel reading is from *Matthew*, its last verses (28:16-20). Unlike Luke or John, Matthew's material on resurrection is neither abundant nor complex. It is, however, full and intense. We saw how Matthew begins his narration in the text examined for Year A at the Vigil. The passage includes Jesus appearing to two women as they hurry away from the tomb. In the gospel that scene is followed by the story of the chief priests concocting a lie to explain the empty tomb (read on Monday of the Octave). The only other scene of resurrection in Matthew's Gospel is the one read here in the Ascension liturgy.

I just spoke of Jesus "being taken up into heaven" as a seeming absence that in reality is a new kind of presence. The scene proclaimed today in Matthew's Gospel expresses this in a slightly different way. It is the only appearance of the risen Jesus to his disciples that Matthew reports—or perhaps better put: Matthew condenses the mystery of the Lord's resurrection appearances into just this single intense scene. There is no indication of the time frame in which what is reported takes place. We hear simply that "the eleven disciples went to Galilee, to the mountain to which Jesus had ordered them." We note that this is Galilee, not Jerusalem, where Luke places his being "taken from them." We hear, "When they saw him, they worshiped, but they doubted." This is an extremely condensed version of scenes developed at greater length in Luke and John and in the longer ending of Mark (Matt 28:8-10; Luke 24:11, 24, 37-41; John 20:24-29; Mark 16:11, 14). But the essential point is made: it is an appearance that provokes the response of worship together with struggle to believe.

Next we hear, "Then Jesus approached and said to them . . ." Jesus appears as one coming. From where? He appears all glorious. They worship him and doubt. He declares, "All power in heaven and on earth has been given to me." That is, he has been established in a position of universal significance. What has happened to "the Crucified" in the resurrection extends its sway into every corner of the cosmos. Then he commissions these disciples, even as some doubted. They are to "make disciples of all nations," precisely because what has happened is of universal significance. They are to baptize "in the name of the Father, and of the Son, and of the Holy Spirit" and they are to teach the nations "to observe all that I have commanded you." Jesus' words here are unique to Matthew's account. Baptism in the name of the Father and the Son and the Holy Spirit combined with transmitting Jesus' teaching become the way that the Lord himself establishes extending his resurrection reality to all nations. It has deeply marked the church ever since. Baptism in the name of the Trinity, at the command of the risen Lord, is the very concrete means of access to the risen presence of Jesus for all.

Jesus' last words confirm this presence. They are amazing and contain a promise, immense in its consolation and scope. He says, "And behold, I am with you always, until the end of the age." Matthew ends his entire gospel here, with these powerful words never ceasing to sound in the ears and hearts of every believer. There is no Jesus being lifted up or taken from sight in Matthew's telling. On Ascension day, in our assembly, as we celebrate the feast, Jesus is the One who comes, and he says, "[B]ehold, I am with you always, until the end of the age," and the words are fulfilled in us as we hear them proclaimed. And as we remember them again and again in our daily lives. This is the new form of presence that begins for us on Ascension day.

In Year B the gospel reading is from *Mark*, verses from the "longer ending," which we spoke about in discussing the gospel text for Saturday in the Octave. The first verse of this Ascension gospel is the last verse of the passage read on that Saturday. Granted, no one, nearly forty days later, is likely to remember that; but it is useful nonetheless to see the rationale for the Lectionary's arrangement. In commenting on the passage read on Saturday of the Octave, I suggested that these verses reflect an author with a knowledge of various resurrection stories in the different gospels. The same observation applies to the verses to be read on Ascension. We hear the words of Jesus to his disciples just before he is taken up into heaven. That Jesus leaves a final message just before this is common to all the gospel accounts and to Acts. The words here are a commission to go into the whole world and proclaim the Gospel "to every creature," an expression unique to this longer Markan ending, as we already observed. There is mention of baptism, something we hear in Matthew's text but not in Luke's. Also unique to this Markan text are the words of Jesus that declare that certain signs will accompany those who believe. The signs are unusual in that no other resurrection text speaks in such terms: driving out demons, speaking new languages, picking up snakes and being unharmed by them or by any deadly drink. Finally, cures of the sick will come about through the laying on of hands.

It is the final verses of this passage that I find especially moving on Ascension day. We hear a sentence that is not heard in any of the other gospels: "So then the Lord Jesus, after he spoke to them, was taken up into heaven and took his seat at the right hand of God." "Lord Jesus" is not a title used anywhere else in Mark or in Matthew. We noted it in Luke's scene at the tomb (Luke 24:3). That Jesus is taken up to heaven is similar to Luke's language in the gospel and in Acts, but only here do we have the further image of him "taking his seat at the right hand of God"—a different image for the mystery of the Ascension, showing that Jesus is completely established in the realm where God is. In the last verse we hear of the disciples going forth and preaching everywhere. In Matthew and Luke the disciples are commissioned to do the same, but none of their accounts reports that happening in the very next verse. Finally, something striking is said about Jesus' continued presence with them even though he is at the right hand of God. We hear, "But they went forth and preached everywhere, while the Lord worked with them and confirmed the word through accompanying signs." We note that Jesus is called "the Lord," and that he is present to them by somehow working with them and confirming their word. This is not unlike Matthew's "Behold, I am with you always, until the end of the age." Nonetheless, it is somehow more specific and less open ended than Matthew's text.

In Year C the gospel reading is from *Luke*, the last verses of that gospel (Luke 24:46-53). It is the continuation of Luke's comparatively complex narration of resurrection appearances that we examined as the gospel passages for Wednesday and Thursday of the Octave, also used as the gospel on the Third Sunday of Easter in Years A and B. Again, it is useful to note the Lectionary's rationale for picking up the text of those earlier uses and placing this ending of Luke's gospel here on Ascension day.

A theme touched upon again and again throughout this book is heard in Jesus' own words at the beginning of this passage: "Thus it is written that the Christ would suffer and rise from the dead on the third day . . ." This is death and resurrection held tightly together and seen as the deepest sense of the Scriptures. But there is more in the words of Jesus that follow. The fruit of his death and resurrection is specified as a content to be preached: ". . . and that repentance, for the forgiveness of sins, would be preached in his name to all the nations, beginning from Jerusalem. You are witnesses of these things." There follows something unique to Luke, both here in his gospel and in the scene in Acts that parallels this. It is Jesus' command that they stay in Jerusalem until they "are clothed with power from on high." Jesus calls this "the promise of my Father" that he will send.

After this there is a change of place. Jesus and the disciples leave the room where they have been gathered. In just a few succinct phrases Luke manages to sketch an amazing scene. As if in procession, Jesus is said to have "led them out as far as Bethany." Then he "raised his hands, and blessed them . . . and was taken up to heaven." An amazing amount of things seems to happen very quickly, or at least to be said very quickly. Not long before in the gospel Jesus is speaking at some length with his overjoyed disciples and even taking something to eat in their presence. Suddenly they are led outside to the edge of the city, Jesus blesses them, and he is taken up to heaven. Strikingly, there is no sadness or disappointment here. We have the short phrase of Luke describing their immediate reaction—"[t]hey did him homage"—and their continued reaction—"they returned to Jerusalem with great joy, and they were continually in the temple praising God."

As we hear this gospel proclaimed on Ascension day, these last verses converge with our present moment of prayer. That same great joy is given to us. It is not a joy that we are meant somehow to conjure up within ourselves. It is given us as the risen Lord's gift. This is what Word and Sacrament deliver. The disciples being continually in the temple praising God is continued now in our own praise. Like them, we do homage to our risen and ascended Lord.

Matthew, Mark, and Luke in Years A, B, and C for the solemnity of the Ascension—in Matthew the scene takes place in Galilee and no time frame is mentioned; in Mark no place is specified and no time; in Luke it takes place in Jerusalem and on the same Sunday of resurrection itself. In Acts the scene is in Jerusalem forty days later. This is, as we have seen, the refusal of the texts to let themselves be tamed into a simple, single, consistent chronological narrative. This is the reality of resurrection and ascension transcending time and place while being present within them. This is ultimately joy for us, as it was for the first witnesses of these events. This too, as for them, is our time and space of worship.

Options for the Second Reading

I mentioned the first reading is always the opening verses of the Acts of the Apostles, in all three years of the cycle. The gospel varies, as we have just noted. The second reading also varies according to the year. There are two different passages from the Letter to the Ephesians in Years A and B and a passage from the Letter to the Hebrews in Year C. All these are very dense theologically. This is an embarrassment of riches for our reflections on what Ascension means. I will just offer one key point from each of these readings, making the effort to be concise but at least suggesting a path for further theological exploration.

In Year A, the passage is Ephesians 1:17-23, but this same passage may also be read in Years B and C. This suggests there is something fundamental about it. The text is a prayer or a wish that Paul offers for the Ephesians. Its proclamation in the liturgy has the direct effect of its being heard as immediately concerning us. Paul prays that "the God of our Lord Jesus Christ, the Father of glory, give [us] a Spirit of wisdom and revelation resulting in knowledge of him." The phrases that follow are profuse and well worth careful meditation, one by one. But their center speaks of our knowing a "surpassing greatness of his power" at work in us. What follows is staggering, for the power at work in us is defined as the same power that God "worked in Christ, raising him from the dead and seating him at his right hand in the heavens." This is uttered as if it were familiar, already well known, describing in the same breath Jesus' resurrection from the dead and his being glorified in heaven. What is fresh and new in the passage is the force with which Paul makes the point that the same power is at work in us and for us. This is why we can rejoice in the Ascension. It is not Jesus going away from us. We feel ourselves drawn up in resurrection with him and taken already to heaven with him precisely by means of the surpassing greatness of God's power at work in us here and now. The passage finishes with a stunning image of all things being put under Christ's feet and Christ filling all things in every way. Ascension is the presence of the risen Christ pervading all the universe!

In Year B another passage from the same letter, Ephesians 4:1-13, is offered as a possibility. These verses likewise are very dense. Prying open the meaning of a psalm verse, Paul sees Psalm 68:19 fulfilled in Christ's ascension. That verse says, "He ascended on high and took prisoners captive; / he gave gifts to men." With this as his basis, Paul sketches out a marvelous image of Christ descending "into the lower regions of the earth" and ascending "far above all the heavens, that he might fill all things." Here again we see the image of Christ's ascending movement filling all things. Taking the psalm as a cue, Paul says that as Christ ascends, he is passing out gifts "for building up the body of Christ," which again, of course, includes us. Christ's ascension involves gifts flowing out from him that build us all into his one body. It appears to be a progressive process that is reaching toward all of us somehow being built up and taken up together into what he calls "the full stature of Christ."

In Year C a passage from the Letter to the Hebrews can be read. This offers a different theological thought world with which to enter the Ascension mystery. Perhaps surprisingly, the image and language of "resurrection" does not occur in Hebrews. This can go unnoticed because we read Hebrews as part of the whole New Testament canon, and so we naturally tend to conflate its language with the other images and language which refer in various ways to the glorification of the crucified Jesus. There is nothing wrong with this tendency. Nevertheless, to read any New Testament book also as a discrete statement of its own can help us catch unique insights.

What do we find instead? The language typical of this letter occurs in its opening verses, which describe the divine son through whom God spoke "in these last days." The son is first described in what we could call his pre-incarnate condition. God has made this son "heir of all things" and is one "through whom he created the universe / who is the refulgence of his glory, the very imprint of his being, / and who sustains all things by his mighty word" (Heb 1:2-3). Clearly the one spoken of here is divine and yet distinguished from God and one through whom God speaks. But it is especially the next verse that interests us as we consider the Ascension. The whole incarnate work of this son is condensed into one short phrase that expresses, with language different from what we have encountered so far, cross and glorification. We read, "When he had accomplished purification from sins [cross], / he took his seat at the right hand of the Majesty on high [glorification] . . ." (Heb 1:4).

This scheme that opens Hebrews is carried consistently through the whole book, and a profound theological understanding of cross and glorification is worked out within this framework. There is no sense of a period of resurrection appearances that eventually closes with Jesus' further glorification and being taken up into heaven. Rather, in the theological world of this letter (worked out especially in chapters 4–10) the death of Jesus is one with what is called Jesus' entry into a heavenly sanctuary. By his death he enters that sanctuary with his own cross as a perfect sacrifice and sprinkles his own blood as a purification of our sins. This entry into the sanctuary by his death *is* his glorification.

The short passage offered for the liturgy of the Ascension takes place well into this development and places together two passages from chapters 9 and 10. We see easily, of course, how the verse just cited from the opening fits well with Ascension. We can say of Jesus that "he took his seat at the right hand of the Majesty on high." Now we can note several verses of the reading that make clear why they are chosen for this day. The passage opens with these words: "Christ did not enter into a sanctuary made by hands, a copy of the true one, but heaven itself, that he might now appear before God on our behalf." As we've seen, this reading was preceded by the vivid passage from Acts 1, that concludes with the image of the "men of Galilee" looking into the sky where a cloud has just taken Jesus from their sight. This verse from Hebrews explains this theologically. Christ enters heaven to appear before God on our behalf. Once again we feel joy in Jesus being taken from our sight.

The passage moves on to a conclusion, saying, "Therefore, brothers and sisters, since through the blood of Jesus we have confidence of entrance into the sanctuary . . . let us approach with a sincere heart and in absolute trust." Note its crucial premise—that *Christ's* entry into the heavenly sanctuary for us implies that we can have confidence of *our own* entrance into sanctuary—and the exhortation that flows from it. . . . Christ *and* us entering the heavenly sanctuary—this is the joyful feast of Ascension that we celebrate!

We can conclude our discussion of these rich and varied Scripture passages on the mystery of the Ascension with just a few words about the liturgy of the Eucharist that follows them. The prayer over the gifts for the Vigil Mass of the Ascension directly makes a link between what we have just examined from Hebrews and the Eucharistic liturgy. It prays, "O God, whose Only Begotten Son, our High Priest, is seated ever-living at your right hand to intercede for us, grant that we may approach with confidence the throne of grace and there obtain your mercy." That approach to the throne of grace is what occurs here and now for us in the celebration of the Eucharist. We are celebrating the Eucharist in some particular place on earth, but that earthly place converges with the heavenly place where Christ is forever interceding for us. We do not need to decide whether we are in heaven or on earth. It is both at once, for the ascended Christ "fills all things in every way" (Eph 1:23). The preface continues this point, prayerfully exclaiming that Christ "ascended, not to distance himself from our lowly state but that we, his members, might be confident of following where he, our Head and Founder, has gone before."

The Missal suggests as the communion antiphon this day the words of Jesus from Matthew's text examined above: "Behold, I am with you always, even to the end of the age, alleluia" (Matt 28:30). The reception of the Lord's Body and Blood to the accompaniment of these words is their strongest fulfillment. Our minds are full of all sorts of images now: the Lord taken from our sight in a cloud, an entrance into a heavenly sanctuary, a being seated at God's right hand, a descending and an ascending, everything being filled, the Body of Christ being built up. No matter which of these images strike us in this movement of prayer, it is his being with us always, even to the end of the age.

Chapter 10

Pentecost Sunday

With the solemnity of Pentecost, the Paschal Mystery is brought to completion. The preface for this day's feast names this as the reason for our giving thanks: "For, bringing the Paschal Mystery to completion, you [God] bestowed the Holy Spirit today . . ." In this final chapter we want to probe the mystery of what it means to declare that the bestowal of the Holy Spirit brings the Paschal Mystery to completion. This also can function as a conclusion to the book, a bringing to completion of these reflections.

I began the reflections on Ascension by referring to what I called the resurrection-ascension nexus. We saw how Luke spread out in a scheme of forty days various dimensions of the disciples' entirely unexpected experiences of the death of Jesus and his impossible-to-categorize resurrection. These experiences and reactions are in fact differently represented in other gospels and other genres of speaking about death and resurrection. We saw that no neatly coherent chronology of events can be established on the basis of the texts. The texts refuse to give this because the reality they refer to transcends what narrative can produce. In any case, we noted that after the death of Jesus there was a period of time, not very long, in which his disciples were in crisis. This was followed by another period in which the crucified Jesus appeared to his disciples, showing himself alive and thus vindicated by his Father. These appearances after a short time came to an end, and Luke's account of ascension represents this in dramatic form. This form has deeply marked the imagination of the church, especially as this scheme began to shape an annual liturgical cycle.

Something similar is true of Luke's presentation of Pentecost. Now we can refer to a resurrection-ascension-pentecost nexus. The Pentecost end of this continuum represents what we earlier described as the discouraged band of disciples being transformed into fearless witnesses of Jesus' resurrection. How did that transformation come about? Again, Luke represents this in dramatic form, spread out ten days after Jesus' ascension or fifty days from his resurrection. This is the completion of the Paschal Mystery, the "hour" of Jesus, the awesome deed of God in its continually unfolding dimensions. Once again, we examine the scriptural texts as the liturgy uses them.

A Reading from the Acts of the Apostles

The first reading is from the Acts of the Apostles (2:1-11) and functions in the Pentecost liturgy in a way similar to how we saw a previous passage from Acts functioning in the Ascension liturgy. We observed there that the narrative weight of the feast is carried by this first reading rather than by the gospel, as is usually the case. Luke's narrative in Acts delivers more details of the Ascension than any gospel text. Something similar is true for the descent of the Holy Spirit on Pentecost; this passage from Acts 2 is the only biblical text that recounts the coming of the Holy Spirit in this way.

To understand it, we should recall several phrases from the passage read on Ascension. In the biblical book they are tightly joined to each other, separated only by the scene of the choice of Matthias to replace Judas (Acts 1:15-26). On Ascension we heard the risen Jesus, just before he was taken from their sight, instructing his apostles to ". . . wait for 'the promise of the Father about which you have heard me speak; for John baptized with water, but in a few days you will be baptized with the Holy Spirit.'" Shortly after this he says, "You will receive power when the Holy Spirit comes upon you, and you will be my witnesses in Jerusalem, throughout Judea and Samaria, and to the ends of the earth." These words are the links in the ascension-pentecost nexus.

Jesus' words are fulfilled in the scene described in the Pentecost reading, and indeed, in the whole rest of the book, which develops under the force of the Holy Spirit given in that scene. What is described there has very much marked Christian imagination and iconography, just as the Ascension scene has done. So it is perhaps surprising to note that the descent of the Spirit is described in only four short verses (Acts 2:1-4). Only a few essential details are given.

First, the apostles, with their number brought back to twelve by the addition of Matthias, are gathered in one place. What happens takes place "suddenly," a word suggesting the surprise the event engenders. A "noise" that is likened to "a strong driving wind" comes from the sky and fills the entire house where they are sitting. On the heels of this noise something strange appears to them: "tongues as of fire, which parted and came to rest on each of them." What this noise and strange vision mean is explained in the next verse: "And they were all filled with the Holy Spirit . . ." This is what Jesus had spoken of just before the Ascension—"the promise of the Father," the being "baptized in the Holy Spirit," the receiving "power when the Holy Spirit comes upon you."

It is striking that the first sign of the Spirit's descent is inspired speech in the disciples. This is the moment they are transformed from having encountered the risen Jesus to becoming effective witnesses of this encounter. In the short passage read in the liturgy on this day, the scene that immediately follows is the gathering of a carefully delineated crowd. They are "devout Jews from every nation under heaven staying in Jerusalem." (Some fourteen different nations or cities are named in Acts 2:9-10.) As Luke tells it, this is no accident but part of the divinely arranged scene. These Jews from every part of the world are themselves brought to Jerusalem by God's design and drawn to this scene by the sound of the loud noise. These will be the first to hear the speech which the Holy Spirit inspires. At the beginning "they were confused because each one heard them speaking in his own language." This is God's doing through the Spirit, reuniting the world divided by different languages from the time of the tower of Babel to this moment. The text summarizes the content of what each one heard in his own language: "we hear them speaking in our own tongues of the mighty acts of God."

This is where the reading finishes. But it is helpful to remind ourselves where Acts goes from here. In effect the whole rest of the book develops from this moment. Moreover, within this same scene Peter next stands up and addresses the crowd. What he says is developed at some length and is a fundamental presentation of the core of the apostolic kerygma. In fact it is the first of those texts that we examined beginning at the day Mass on the Sunday of Resurrection and extending through the days of the Octave, the texts with the variations on the core theme, "This Jesus whom you crucified, God has raised him up." Jesus being crucified and his being raised up are the "mighty acts of God" which the apostles, filled with the Holy Spirit, have been "enabled to proclaim." (See above, pp. 105–7, 113–14, on Easter day, Acts 10:34, 37-43, and "Readings from Acts during the Octave of Easter.")

It is significant that, as Luke emphasizes, Jews gathered in Jerusalem from every part of the world will be the first people to whom the apostolic preaching is addressed, proclaiming that "God has made both Lord and Messiah this Jesus whom you crucified" (Acts 2:36). This scheme for the Gospel being preached first to Jews is carried through to the end of chapter 7 of Acts. These chapters all show that in Jesus being made Lord and Messiah, God has been faithful to his promises to Israel. Many Jews come to believe. Then beginning in chapter 8, the Gospel message is taken, according to the geographical itinerary announced by Jesus in Acts 1:8, "throughout Judea and Samaria, and to the ends of the earth." The book ends with the Gospel reaching Rome through Paul (Acts 28:14-31).

In any case, the Gospel reaching from Jerusalem to the ends of the earth begins here on the day of Pentecost. And that is part of what we now are celebrating and praying about for ourselves in our own celebration of the feast. The collect for the Mass of this day is imbued with all these themes. It addresses God as one "who by the mystery of today's great feast sanctify your whole Church in every people and nation . . ." It is on the basis of what God did on the original day of Pentecost that we dare to ask for something similar in our present day: ". . . pour out, we pray, the gifts of the Holy Spirit across the face of the earth . . ." The worldwide scope of what we ask for is inspired by the original scope of the Pentecost event. We are still praying for everyone in the last petition of the prayer, but it is formulated in such a way that we see we are praying also very much for ourselves. Still referring to this original Pentecost, we ask, "with the divine grace that was at work when the Gospel was first proclaimed, fill now once more the hearts of believers."

Throughout this book I have claimed that the proclamation of the Sacred Scripture in any given liturgy is a revelation of the event of that liturgy in the concrete community that is celebrating it. It is a revelation of the feast. And so on Pentecost a community becomes aware that today *is* Pentecost, Pentecost here and now in the liturgy being celebrated, the Paschal Mystery being brought to completion in this community. The Scriptures declare what is happening: "[S]uddenly there came from the sky a noise like a strong driving wind, and it filled the entire house in which they were." The text that recounts the past converges with our present, and we can say that our faith detects that tongues as of fire settle on each one of us. And all of us too are "filled with the Holy Spirit" and are enabled to proclaim the mighty acts of God. Throughout the whole liturgy we proclaim these, and then, marked by this liturgical experience, we proclaim the same by our deeds and words in the world.

An Option for the Second Reading

But what does it mean to say that all of us are "filled with the Holy Spirit"? One of the options offered for the second reading, Romans 8:8-17, provides a clear answer. "But you are not in the flesh," Paul says. "[O]n the contrary, you are in the spirit, if only the Spirit of God dwells in you." He goes on to describe what the Spirit does in us: "If the Spirit of the one who raised Jesus from the dead dwells in you, the one who raised Christ from the dead will give life to your mortal bodies also, through his Spirit that dwells in you." This is a stunning claim. We note the trinitarian dimensions of his explanation. The "one who raised Jesus from the dead" is the Father, and his Spirit is at work in us doing the very same that he did in the Son—namely, giving life to our mortal bodies "through his Spirit that dwells" in us.

It is "a Spirit of adoption." This means that the Spirit gives to us the same relationship with God the Father that has belonged to the Son from all eternity. St. Paul says, "[Y]ou received a Spirit of adoption, through whom we cry, 'Abba, Father!'" This is the fundamental shape of all our liturgical prayer. St. Paul says, "The Spirit himself bears witness with our spirit that we are children of God, and if children, then heirs, heirs of God and joint heirs with Christ."

Pentecost is virtually infinite in its proportions. We are heirs of God! We are joint heirs with Christ! We participate in divine life! We participate in the life of the Trinity! By adoption we live inside the love that Father, Son, and Holy Spirit enjoy among themselves. In the Holy Spirit, and from the place of the Son, *we* cry, "Abba, Father!" This is the shape, this is the form of our entire life. In the Holy Spirit, and from the place of the Son, *we* cry, "Abba, Father!"

There is, however, a condition required for inheriting this divine life, a condition upon which we receive adoption. And it is, says

St. Paul, "if only we suffer with him so that we may also be glorified with him." Once again, cross and resurrection are held in dynamic tension, not only in the proclamation of Jesus but in the shape of our own Christian lives as we are conformed to him.

The Gospel Reading for Pentecost

A different gospel passage is offered on Pentecost for each year of the Lectionary cycle. The gospel in Year A is John 20:19-23, and this can be used in Years B and C as well, an indication that it can be considered the most fundamental or most clearly suited to Pentecost.

It is an effective and suggestive passage to read on the day of Pentecost because it recounts something that, within John's resurrection narratives, happens on the very day of resurrection. Its effect, then, is to connect the giving of the Holy Spirit very tightly to the risen Lord himself. Liturgically the fifty days of the Easter season have spread out and unfolded a mystery and a grace tightly condensed into the resurrection of Jesus. One of the ways we have referred to this is as the resurrection-ascension-pentecost nexus. This nexus is resurrection appearances and instructions that eventually come to an end and a promised gift of the Holy Spirit. All of this is condensed into the short passage from the Gospel of John read now.

The scene opens with the disciples hiding in fear behind locked doors. Here is evidence of their crisis at the death of Jesus. Unexpectedly the risen Jesus "came and stood in their midst and said to them, 'Peace be with you.'" This is followed by what may be considered an instructive dimension of the appearance. "He showed them his hands and his side," which teaches them in effect that the one they are seeing is the one who was crucified and whose side was opened by a soldier's lance. We are told succinctly that "The disciples rejoiced when they saw the Lord." What happens next shows why the passage would be selected for Pentecost. We read, "Jesus said to them again, 'Peace be with you. As the Father has sent me, so I send you.' And when he had said this, he breathed on them and said to them, 'Receive the Holy Spirit. Whose sins you forgive are forgiven them, and whose sins you retain are retained.'"

There is something thrilling in all this. First of all, there is Jesus' repeated greeting of peace. There are no recriminations for their having abandoned him, no reproaches, no scoldings. There is only his peace-filled greeting and their joy. But this is followed immediately by a profound commissioning. Jesus says, "*As* the Father has sent me, *so* I send you." This is enormous. Glorious, divine, powerful, creative, peaceful was the Father's sending of his Son into the world. And now—as the gospel's words converge with our present celebration of the liturgy—*we* are sent by Jesus in the same way. And for this profound task, he breathes on us the gift of the Holy Spirit. It is marvelous to see the Holy Spirit coming out of the body of the risen Lord, the body marked by wounds in its hands, feet, and side. We have an image here of basically every theme I have tried to emphasize throughout this book. The risen body bearing the marks of crucifixion holds cross and resurrection in perfect tension. The Holy Spirit delivered by the breath of the body of the risen Lord and effecting a commission shows the gift of the Holy Spirit rooted in the death and resurrection of Jesus. Without the text saying so, Jesus vanishes from their sight as soon as the Spirit is breathed out on the disciples. This is the resurrection-ascension-pentecost nexus, not spread out over fifty days, but condensed into one intense scene of an appearance and a withdrawal on the very day of resurrection.

But what does Jesus' withdrawal from our sight mean? This breath of the risen Lord never ceases. The first day and the fiftieth day and today—for us with faith, they are all the same: the new everlasting day of resurrection, the new everlasting day of Pentecost. The presence of the risen Jesus and his act of breathing on his disciples never ceases in the church. And in this way resurrection creates mission. Jesus breathes the Holy Spirit onto us and sends us just as he was sent. He has given us everything that he has from the Father. And so this mission has a content—the forgiveness of sins. "Receive the Holy Spirit," he says to those whom he sends. "Whose sins you forgive are forgiven them, and whose sins you retain are retained." The forgiveness of sins is the first fruit of the resurrection. "He showed them his hands and his side." From this crucified now risen body, from his glorious wounds, there is in the church, his Body, an unceasing outpouring of the Holy Spirit for mission and for the forgiveness of sins.

The Lectionary offers other options for gospel readings on the feast of Pentecost and other options for second readings that I have not treated here. In addition, the Lectionary and the Missal offer biblical texts from the Old Testament and prayers to accompany them for an extended Vigil Mass of Pentecost, echoing in part the extended Paschal Vigil. These biblical passages and prayers are an embarrassment of riches even more abundant than the one noted for Ascension, where I attempted to comment on all at least briefly. That is not possible here. Nonetheless, I would like to offer just a few more remarks to conclude what I have been referring to as the liturgical event of our Pentecost.

The Epiclesis of the Eucharistic Liturgy

The day when the gift of the Holy Spirit is lavishly poured out on the church seems to be an apt place to make at least a brief remark about that part of the eucharistic prayer called "epiclesis," a Greek word which has become technical liturgical vocabulary for that moment in liturgy when the Holy Spirit is invoked and is poured out. (I have reflected on this at some length in other writings. See *What Happens at Mass*, pp. 83–86 and 94–96, or *Theology at the Eucharistic Table*, pp. 165–74.)[1] The Eucharist is the greatest, most sublime gift given us by the Holy Spirit. The Eucharist is the guarantee and confirmation of all that I have been saying, not only in this chapter but throughout this book. In the Eucharist, the Holy Spirit, who is the definitive author of the Sacred Scriptures, acts within us in such a way that the words are alive with a divine power. The Spirit, author of the sacraments—his masterpieces!—acts in such a way that the Father and the Son take up their dwelling within us by means of the transformation of bread and wine into the Body and Blood of Christ. Every word, every gesture, every movement of the eucharistic liturgy effects and reveals that *we* are made the resplendent dwelling place of the Father and the Son by the working of the Holy Spirit.

When the priest extends his hands over the gifts and implores the Father, "by the same Spirit graciously make holy these gifts . . . that they may become the Body and Blood of your Son our Lord Jesus Christ . . . ," in that same moment Jesus—ascended—is praying to his Father to send the Holy Spirit to us, and the Father responds immediately! Again, when the priest prays to the Father "that we, who are nourished by the Body and Blood of your Son and filled with his Holy Spirit, may become one body, one spirit in Christ," it is through

---

1. Jeremy Driscoll, *What Happens at Mass*, rev. ed. (Chicago: Liturgy Training Publications, 2011); Driscoll, *Theology at the Eucharistic Table: Master Themes in the Theological Tradition* (Herefordshire, UK: Gracewing, 2005).

our ascended Lord that this prayer is made to the Father, and the Father responds immediately. And so in fact now we, filled with the Holy Spirit, do become one body, one spirit in Christ.

The Communion Antiphon for Pentecost

The Roman Missal envisions the congregation coming forward for Holy Communion on Pentecost while singing words taken from the account in Acts that formed part of the first reading: "They were all filled with the Holy Spirit and spoke of the marvels of God, alleluia." To receive the Body and Blood of *Christ* is to receive the Holy *Spirit*, the promised gift of the *Father*. The work of the Holy Trinity is now fully manifest. Eucharist *is* Pentecost! On the Today of the feast and on every Today. The Spirit is always with us, and thus the Paschal Mystery is brought to completion.

And so this book reaches a quiet finish, the kind of quiet so typical of the work of God, who is manifest in "a tiny whispering sound" (1 Kgs 19:12). In the Holy Spirit—gift of the Father—the crucified and risen Lord Jesus—gift of the Father—is forever alive in those who put their faith in him.

Immolatus iam non moritur.
Semper vivit occisus.